Shinie Antony is a writer and editor based in Bengaluru. She is the author of several novels and short story collections. Co-founder of the Bangalore Literature Festival and director of the Bengaluru Poetry Festival, her story, 'A Dog's Death', won the Commonwealth Short Story Asia prize in 2002. Her columns appear in *The Times of India*, *The New Indian Express* and CNBC.

ALSO BY SHINIE ANTONY

Novels

Eden Abandoned: The Story of Lilith
The Girl Who Couldn't Love
When Mira Went Forth and Multiplied
A Kingdom for his Love

Short Fiction

Barefoot and Pregnant
The Orphanage for Words

Anthologies (Edited)

Boo
Why We Don't Talk
An Unsuitable Woman

can't

A Novel

Shinie Antony

SPEAKING TIGER

SPEAKING TIGER BOOKS LLP
125A, Ground Floor, Shahpur Jat, near Asiad Village,
New Delhi 110049

First published by Speaking Tiger Books 2024

ISBN: 978-93-5447-660-0
eISBN: 978-93-5447-659-4

10 9 8 7 6 5 4 3 2 1

Typeset in Sabon Roman by SÜRYA, New Delhi
Printed at HT Media Ltd, Greater Noida

'Go to sleep in the water face down /
pulling the sea over my head.'

—tata

1

IT SHOCKED MOST people those days, her casual mentions of her husband's affairs. Not that the married were terribly faithful even back then but no one except her said so. And said in that laughing, lilting way, as if infidelity was a joke between wife and the other woman.

Her stories were never-ending, inexhaustible. The husband's pants fell off again, again, again. No one could claim to have heard the last of it, there was always one more funny story she was going to tell. She'd leave in her wake a whiff of scandal, of the illicit, of betrayal and a monumental wholesome forgiveness, like other women of her times left behind their piety or imported perfume.

'*Someone*,' she'd begin, 'was caught in the pantry with a cook...'

This promise of salacious detail, of another stray incident from her past, steamy yet oh so moral—she was always cheated on, never cheating—made Nena a delicious oddity in these parts. Though her exact age was unknown, none thought her a day younger than seventy—there was nothing you could tell her that she hadn't heard before. They went to her with their doubts and dilemmas, and she, in turn, gave them a story, a first-person account they were at liberty to believe or not. They tried their best to pity her—for she lived alone, without husband or son—but were sidetracked by her ear-splitting laugh. She had once been spotted on a bridge staring down at the surf in a wonder-struck way, which gave rise to some talk about the possibility of her ending it all but whoever spoke to her reported back such obscene mirth—that a dull thing like suicide was eventually thought beneath her.

I think I'd heard her, when still a little boy dangled by my mother's finger, sum up her general philosophy of life. 'Who cares?' she said, laughing so infectious a laugh that lepers nearby forgot to ask for alms. She seemed to descend on lesser mortals slanted as the rain; everyone stopped talking, feeling a little foolish, a little garrulous, as she approached. This was a small town but there was something so broadminded about her, so well-travelled—a fledgling seer left behind by migratory mystics for a lark.

~

I was home at summer's peak, my sudden reappearance blotting the sun from my mother's sky. Our warfare showed no sign of abating. Dropping out of class when she'd have to continue paying good money to retain my seat in a fancy college out of town forced her to bring up the matter of her widowhood and meagre means on a daily basis. I was born on the day of my father's funeral with a dim memory of him head-butting her womb. You clawed out of me before I could grieve, was a steady nagging of hers, she who hatched eggs in a marriage full of rage.

My poor father, who worked hard for the paltry money he made. My poor mother, who got barely enough to eat the nine months I was under construction. Nothing in their lives before my arrival is hidden from me. He hit her, he hit me. She curled up on the floor like me in her womb, bled into bunched up rags, went into labour. But that day, the day I started to unwind out of her, he held his heart and collapsed under the noon sun. We were back, my mother and I, in time for his funeral. The midwife still held the needle in her hand, my mother was fond of saying.

I'm an inauspicious person, if you want to look at me that way. I killed my own father, you could say that too. The placenta fed me my mother's stoic silence, my father's violence. I let the air go by without breathing.

Each era sees a new insolence, a vanity of its own. For my mother and the women of her acquaintance praying was how they'd save the world, their worship not just for themselves but for everyone. They woke up before dawn, squared their shoulders and on empty sacrificing stomachs quarrelled with God on our behalf. Cheap reproductions of religious paintings and statuettes of gods made up the walls of our one-room tenement. Lungs lined with the ash of joss sticks, we undertook rigorous fasts and barefoot treks, eating only fruit, drinking only milk, abruptly shaving off hair to appease a passing god. My mother prayed on payment; people queued up with requests to their late ancestors since she claimed trances transported her to the grainy twilight between the living and the dead. And when she wasn't praying for mankind or lost cattle, she was praying for me.

Every prayer that left her lips fixed its hands around my neck, squeezing, squeezing. Given to moaning about her kismet, her fate, her stars, her bad luck, black future, the messy knot of lines on her palm—against all of which she only had her only son, me. A son who in the absence of husbands was the spare arrow in her patriarchal quiver, but whose lack of voice disturbed her not only during devotional songs but also dinner conversations. This speech impediment was the first sign she misinterpreted as a sign of divine wrath. Only when I strung together sounds for the first time at the age of ten did she stop running out barefoot to self-flagellate on fiery cobblestones.

Silence is my first language, my mother tongue. I don't trust words—words take sides. Not that I am spineless, mind. Just that my spine's split, loyal to two at once. I was her son; I was also I, whoever that be. Angular, insomniac, owl of skin and bone, carrying with me my own stink, like self-contained sewage.

When my mother opened the door in the middle of the night, she first thought I had died and was my own ghoul, a misunderstanding that cleared once I asked for food. The stonewalling of her shrill questions regarding my return drove her to distraction. She was irritable, foul-mouthed and pitied herself copiously, her bodily discomforts and the burden of me all she could speak of. Then Nena was mentioned. She was as taken in by Nena's air of worldliness as the others. 'You should do something useful with your time, she will know what.'

Nena. The only madwoman our town could boast of. I'd been intrigued enough while growing up, what with her haphazard philanthropy as well as everyone quoting her on the subject of her husband's many women.

If Nena hadn't held my mother's hand after my father died, our tiny two-member family would have fallen apart before this story began. I daresay my mother would've sold herself to sustain me if she had the good health to pass off as human. As it was, she looked rat-nibbled, her hair a frizzy tornado rising from her scalp. But we clung to each other at night, however much we bad-mouthed one another during the day. She clutched me to her bosom and we ran away somewhere together in our dreams.

Sending me to study would have meant servile bondage unto death for my mother had Nena not intervened with legal help and her knowhow of land ceiling acts and rulings, so that, abracadabra, we suddenly had our own itsy-bitsy acre. This my mother mortgaged to pamper me with an education, and this is the education that I had kicked aside so thoughtlessly.

Ushering me before her, my mother was sure to have experienced a sense of defeat, like the godlessness of a stranger was somehow superior to her own high-strung theism. I stood there biting a fingernail, aware of my utter uselessness and also revelling in it, listening to her exalt Nena to the level of a supernatural tailor, someone who could sew soul and skin together. I needed a little hemming, just a little taking in here or here.

~

All the while my mother lamented about me Nena kept a straight face but the minute we were alone she put a finger on her lips, 'Not another word about studies', as if I'd been the one harping on it.

What had I heard of her, she demanded.

Just her name, I said or stammered.

Up close her face seemed to be constructed with features plucked from other faces; a perfect nose, perfect teeth, perfect eyebrows, but somehow not hers. And a dimple so deep it sank the cheek.

She showed me around her home, merely adequate now that I think of it but at the time much roomier than the cramped quarters I shared with my mother, with steep corners where you least expect. The hall, which you entered directly through a front door rarely locked or latched, tried to pass off junk as furniture. Her room, which I could only spy from the hall, held in its fist a large disorderly crumpled heap of bedclothes; if Nena wasn't standing where you could see her, you'd well believe she was somewhere under that mess trying to find her way out. My mother always said drawing rooms were just what people wanted you to think of them—so they decorated and hung up their fancy art there—but kitchens were what they were really like. Nena ushered me into hers with an 'I specifically asked for a house without a kitchen'. A cooking area this sparse and functional made me rethink how rich people lived—without utensils or the splash of running water. Unlike my mother who collected pots and pans discarded by other people and made out of them a small aluminium mountain that clanged and shone. Nena's kitchen was the end of a corridor within two rows of bricks. The stove was set in rough, abrasive stone, with two black-bottomed pans sitting gloomily by. Wooden ladles hung from nails along with knives. Mushrooms sprang out of the cracks on the walls and a ripe jackfruit lay there like an angry doormat. The larder was full of grain sacks, all gaping open at the neck, 'so mice can help themselves'. The tour ended before a lamp of brass and dust. 'Do not touch,' she said, pointing at it sternly, 'or you might make a wish come true.'

We pottered about in her backyard, where she separated weeds patiently from flowers and paused at one point to scold somewhat expectedly, 'How like men, going by looks!'

I'd tensed up in anticipation, not averse to listening about the randy husband, but she chatted on other matters till it was time for me to go. She gave me some tea, lukewarm just as I like it, and sighed without preamble, 'And you a virgin.'

My entire face went into a spasm, I couldn't help it. We are never as sophisticated as we think. 'I am one too, that's how I know,' she continued. 'We virgins feel pain more than the others, you know, than those who touch and are touched. There's something medicinal about sex...Bodies as balm. But you and me, we hurt head to toe.'

I don't recall my response or how much time after this did I leave her home, but it was only when I was in bed on the brink of sleep, when I finally got over the humiliation of my self-broadcasting virginity, that I thought of *her* virginity. Had she said that or did I just make that up? It can't be true! She can't be a virgin! Just before I fell asleep I promised myself I would ask her about it the next day but I never did.

~

The first week she spoke all the time, her mind jumping from one thing to another in a mercurial randomness peculiar to her. After a reasonable amount of time, when we had walked around her garden ruminating over life at length in the most obscure manner, I'd depart. The lazily made tea she forgot to serve in time was my cue to leave. (There would always be one key ingredient missing; jaggery, milk, water or tealeaf—only one though.) 'There it is,' she would say looking behind me mid-sentence, having forgotten where she had placed the cup.

I would retrieve it, place it on my crossed knee and sip slowly as if it hadn't cooled at all. Her half-hearted offers of heating it up I'd repeatedly rebuff. There was that one time she did pick up the cup and reheat the tea but it still reached me room temperature.

Random people dropping in unannounced was routine. They came with an urgent air, seeking her counsel. At such times I was the tea-maker, scrambling among her twin shelves to find all that was needed. She always paused when I served tea, not wanting to give away the nature of their problems—my cue to disappear among her weeds—but her conversation the next day would contain some clue to what had been discussed. She had lived long enough not to find any problem fatal.

A stranger who stopped to admire her garden was sent off with a bouquet hastily thrown together—pipe vines, curumamil, a spider lily. After he left, she said she didn't know how these manipulative strongly scented blooms overtook the thorns she carefully planted; 'Evil always uses too much cologne, don't you think?'

She never let me use the spade for fear I'd cut travelling worms in two. And while I pretended to toil in the overgrowth, she'd be inside pounding dry leaves and seeds, nutmeg and bishop's weed and anything I imagine she wrested out of bird beaks. Humming to herself and stirring a pot, most of her hair hanging out of her bun, she'd bring me a spoonful to taste, and if anyone peeked through the window, we could look like dancers perfecting a step.

It was in August, after her bushes were compost and a wandering goat caught its hind leg in the spiky fence, that she made a reference to her husband at last. As per habit it was completely abrupt. I had straightened the watercolour on her wall—a marmoset monkey drawn with an infatuated grin—when I heard her say, 'The cook, that too.'

I waited. Since she could refer to herself in the third

person from time to time, there was no saying who she meant; 'I think in several languages,' she had told me.

'He said, "Nena, *she* seduced me, taught me the pleasures of the flesh". Imagine! Just imagine!'

(At which open invite I balked. I could not imagine a man so old—husbands were older than their wives in my opinion then, and Nena was ageless to begin with, infinity before and behind her—in an agile position without a stitch on.)

'Paid to enter kitchens. Peel potatoes, shell peas. Nourish.' She took pity on me then, gestured me into a worn-out sofa stuffed, it felt, with broken skulls. Dust flew out of it like startled birds when I sat. She shut her eyes and opened them, all the while the furniture munching and grunting beneath me. Had her eyes always been this big?

'Listen,' she said. In the warped wood of the sofa's arm a termite shifted house.

~

The boy was playing with his friends outside his house. They were playing...Not important what they were playing, is it? He was fourteen or fifteen or sixteen or seventeen, we will never know. His parents lived in another part of the town because they were stone-cutters or professors, one or the other. He himself lived with an aunt who was never home, owing to mysterious but grand reasons. Perhaps she was a spy. Perhaps she was a ghost. 'I have to go,' is all she told the boy, leaving him to make his way to school and then back to an empty house, where standing at the door waiting for him to use the key was The Cook.

A woman of indeterminate age and looks, her height and weight of no consequence here. Hair tangled, hem in tatters. She called out his name on one unspecific day, so that he turned to his friends and raised a hand in farewell. Bounding into the house he could not at first see her, the room dim from the dusk outside. His eyes caught a flutter. And there she was. All of her all at once. Like thunder or lightning. Stark naked.

He had barely time to take this in when she muttered blackly about her husband and his refusal to give her what she desired most, babies. Her mutterings sounded like incantations in a foreign tongue.

'Laughing stock he's made me,' she told him grimly, and he wanted to flee. From all that back story and raw despair; he could smell the tears in her eyes from where he stood. But then he began to look at her body, properly look. It was the first body he ever saw unclothed. There was curiosity, awe, intrigue and then lust sly and shy. Each heartbeat a hue and cry.

Then, once she was his lullaby and his lyre, did he see her again? No. She took herself off as suddenly as she had brought herself to him. Without warning. One fine day. One not so fine day.

For years he dragged her techniques into every bed of his, with many, many women, women who would never be her. Women he saw but once. That's when he felt one with her the most, when he went missing from someone's life wordlessly. He was sadist enough by then to lie back somewhere else, maybe even with someone else, and recreate almost sensually in his mind that look of utter desolation on the woman's face, the woman he had tenderly lain with just last night and left behind deliberately. When heart-soul-body strain in incoherent unison, nothing can equal that pull, right?

He never called her The Cook of course. In his telling she had become Dhoop. She had allowed him to call her that just once. He had told her, borrowing her boldness, I am your lover, love makes us equals. I can call you by your name. I *want* to call you by your name.

She told him names were for ordinary people, for people who were insecure of losing closeness, for those who needed the world's intervention to get by. But between them artifice was the last thing on their minds, in their bodies. Dazzled, he shut up. They called each other nothing, no name, until one day out of the blue she said, 'Dhoop', the word rising like the sun, a voluptuous scald on his skin.

He never saw her again. His aunt, the absconding self-important elderly secret agent/spirit, said to him, 'We will replace Dhoop with a new cook,' which was when he understood that was what she was called. And she had given him her name in farewell, as a resurrection of earthly fences, hierarchies of caste, age and status, between them.

O, his heart, the haemorrhage of it.

Years later, even while being administered to by his wife on what he thought his deathbed, he reached out for his first love, for Dhoop, his tongue lingering on the vowel. She who taught him that to be loved forever you had to leave mid-love, halfway through the loving.

Ache is everything between men and women.

2

I DID NOT repeat this story to my mother, who unfailingly asked me about my day, looking after me expectantly even when I shook my head and walked off. I listed the boring chores; at Nena's I shopped for groceries, handpicked her vegetables, washed them, chopped them. Tended to the nettles, read to her as she was too vain to wear glasses, and cleared the table in case she had snacked there. Since I reached around noon—Nena said she woke up only by twelve—in a couple of hours I'd be done, sitting there with my long skinny arms dangling between my knees. That was when any conversation happened if it had to happen.

After she told me about her husband's first time with a woman there was a lull in the tales. Instead, she adopted a brisk silence, as if rearranging in her head what not to say to me. With the luxury of the long years in between I wonder if Nena being Nena was waiting for me to give in and use what words I knew.

At the time I watched her covertly, without looking, putting her in charge of all communication between us.

Meanwhile, I took over the tea ceremony. I would leave the cups—my chipped one and her leaf-painted one—about exactly like she did. When the food on the windowsill grew mold, I threw it away. Often, I packed the garbage from her house into a neat parcel to dump on my way back. If she caught me at it, she tied a bow around it in farewell. Eye contact was her main currency, two near-sighted eyes curtained by eyelashes of uncommon length, that met yours with the blinding honesty of the sun. Even now (like then) I imagine her going about her house checking doors and desks for a pulse. To her they had blood and bones and bad memories.

~

The absence of stored water never struck me as odd though in my own home my mother hounded me to wash my hands, my feet, my face every chance she got. An old rusted tap at the end of our lane drip-dripped at will, a tap my mother declared her mortal enemy. We filled up barrels and rolled them home without spilling a drop, pirates mid-sea with stolen gold. The kitchen window at Nena's place, latched most of the time, looked down into the deep, narrow neck of a well, the water from which I used in her garden, or what I thought of as her anti-garden. I filled up the terracotta jug in the house, the one with handles on either side, but soon understood that I was the only one drinking from it. The outhouse, which I used sometimes, had the dry-mouthed air of a place expecting ghosts. Unused as I was to musing on anything beyond the immediate, it was only a faint registering at the back of my mind, this surety that the outhouse saw no visitor except me. Where did Nena conduct her ablutions? It was only when I went to her with a bowl of water when she came back with grimy hands from the garden that I heard her on the subject. 'I'm allergic to water,' she said like it was something I should have known. I didn't believe her—who would? These little words that scampered away like nervous kittens.

She held her cup with such force another day that some of the tea jumped into the saucer. She gasped and held her skirt away from her, shushing at it.

I can make you some more, I offered in my servile role.

'Kettles must sleep too.'

Like the first line of a folksong so I waited, but she dragged her heavy-lidded eyes back to me. 'Have you ever seen me *have* tea?'

An overrated beverage, invented as a meaningful pause during conversations, something to take away the awkwardness of having nothing to say, giving the hands something to do. 'You don't take milk,' I murmured.

'Water,' she murmured back. 'I told you I'm allergic to it. Nena, my mother used to say, you spat out breast-milk as if it was vinegar.'

This too I could not relate to my mother. Not because it wasn't extraordinary enough—who on this planet could die from drinking water?—but it was precisely the kind of fact that could be traced back to the only one who knew—me. I keep secrets not out of loyalty but from a reluctance to speak, a shut mouth the only weapon I have.

Another thought struck me. Nena, as far as I noticed, neither washed nor bathed, at least not when I was around, her outdoor bathroom floor dry as a bone. Yet that clean glow to her as if fitted with a halo.

'I soak herbs in water to swallow as pills.' Imparted as I shooed off a pigeon white enough to be a dove, as though she had read my thoughts. 'I scrub myself with all that I powder day and night.'

I kept any skepticism to myself; it seemed like a quaint condition to have, handy to distract anyone with. Some brag about a villa in a vale, some about... eczema. I brought the same gravitas to her that I did to everybody else, except when she was joking, which she did without warning or change of expression. I was careful with my laughs. If I laughed too early or too late, too little or too much, she'd say, as if admiringly, with a gap between the two words: 'So polite!'

One by-product of our now-familiar lengthy silences

and her studied breaking of them was the mutual respect that sprang up between us. I asked nothing except what she supplied. No disbelief, however provocative her confession, widened my eye. By now two things were clear—she was not the whimsical social sparrow she pretended to be and I was not going to be seriously advised on my future anytime soon. Left to ourselves she would have gone on with her unexpected bursts of candour and I'd have maintained this muteness unto death.

The thing about her. Unlike me, who waited for real life to begin tomorrow or day after, next month, next year, a time not now, maybe later or even never, here was she occupying her yesterdays as solidly as she did her todays.

There are many stories, she said, you say which. I had to choose, she insisted, because choices constantly remade us. Mermaids pray for feet or the face of a fish, but one or the other, didn't they?

Tell me, I indicated with a low wave of my hand, the very last one.

~

It won't do, he coldly informed his mirror, growing old together with his reflection simply wasn't an option. He would not let that happen to him! Yes, he had seen others bald, toothless, drooling, defecating in beds. The droop and the drip of them. But he was going to fool Father Time, whose withered scrotum had surely fallen off by now. And he would do this in broad daylight. Not for him wigs and vitamin supplements and crotch-fit pants. He just quietly continued to do what he always had, hoping to catch no one's attention; drank, smoked, and debauched himself beyond limits. He ignored the rubbery lung, the sluggish heart, slippery memory, enlarged prostate and giddy spells first thing in the morning. All parties in that posh part of the world began on his terrace, where a restored confession booth of wood from an old ransacked church in Rome served as both blasphemy and bar.

Every morning he woke up with a new woman and there was a reason for that. There was no dearth of beautiful young girls poor enough to prostitute themselves for five-star scraps. No girl, however, wanted to return to the bed of so genial a man who asked nothing of them. They were not made to piss on him, call a friend to join in, stand upside down. They couldn't even just go to sleep. Instead, they had to watch him cry.

In the middle of the night, after all that trotting about on heels and uncomfortable thongs that rubbed them raw, they were treated to the sight of a grown man who reminded them of their daddy—or a daddy in a movie they watched as a child, the daddy they searched for in every customer—weep like a baby.

Oh, they knew, had they gone about it the regular way, he would arrange for their abortions or send money orders for their little illicit mites back home, but the price he asked of them was too high. They were simply not trained to hold someone's hand in dementia. Nymphs they were, not nurses. Now if he had kept them up at night chatting about who had violated them and how, they'd cheerily have stayed, but this scavenging he tried to do down their soul, no sir! One by one they flew back into the night with their perfectly plucked eyebrows.

The drinking went on but the dancing ceased. It was getting more and more difficult to get a companion for the night. Floozies and tarts and sirens and harlots with hearts of gold, the town had run out of them all. He sat, in his silk dressing gown imported all the way from Italy, entire nights alone on his terrace, a thoroughly ineligible bachelor. He had been married once but... that's a story for another time.

A rustle below. Was there someone in his house? Curious but not too steady, he began his slow descent, one step at a time. He had thrown up earlier—livers were such party poopers—and a drop of something regurgitated clung to his lower lip in a rare shade of brown. As he moved far from nimble towards his room the susurration of tiny bells reached his ear, the right one (the left had long given up). There was someone waiting for him! His entire life flashed before him in a single scene. There were so many, so many memories he wanted to recount, and surprisingly none of them from his stud days. The women he bedded were a blur. His dear mother, he wanted to begin with her, and then that aunt who beat the crap out of him whenever he was scared, whenever he wet the bed, whenever...How he missed the good women in his life!

It felt nice to make his way slow and steady like this, with such spectacular hope in heart, sure that The One had finally come to him.

He well knew how lucky he had been when it came to women. (He thought of them as a heap of feathered things in his backyard, chirping away, their baubles and beads catching the light now and then.) He had only to wish for one and she would be granted to him in a way that suited him best. Everything about women pleased him. Their little ears, their big fat love, startled necks with ostrich napes, their moans and gasping cries, the words that escaped them in anger and amour. That look in their eyes when they first realised they loved you, only you. Which only intensified when they knew you didn't, couldn't, wouldn't love them back.

He was beginning to realise that he may not be able to reach the room after all; his shin was sciatic and hip numb. Don't ask him about his legs, like losing two of your most patriotic soldiers below the waist. This was tiresome, he complained to himself. He would have so liked to invite a new companion into his life. He tried to call out but his lower denture was still in the ashtray upstairs; without teeth his words were just plops. Plus, he was afraid he was going to soil himself.

A flurry of footsteps and there, at last, stood the guest. In anklets, bracelets, the shortest dress you ever saw and the reddest lips you never kissed. A boy-girl, or a birl as he called them, these little chappies who were the most luscious girlie-girl on the inside but still boy o' boy on the outside.

You know what, he said, I love you.

The birl twirled closer, not having bargained for a slithering host. I love you too, he/she said, for that seemed an apt thing to say in the middle of robbing a house.

'Will you hug me just a little?'

The birl twirled yet closer, his/her hand hovering on the man's chest. Then he/she bent and scooped the older man into his muscular arms, carried him to his bed and tucked him into it. He/she sat by the bedside, head cocked to one side in a classic listening pose. Two wings, one pink and one blue, undulated off his/her shoulder blades.

They sat like that, holding hands, swapping reminiscences, turtle to tiger/tigress. The frock did not come off, no stains on sheet, but something happened that night. Just before the old man fell asleep, he fell in love for the nth time.

When he woke up no one was in the room. A

faint memory came to him, of other-worldly beings in inappropriate clothing, of unconditional love sans genitalia and the outpouring of every regret, every remorse in his heart. He had an idea then that this was going to be his grand-finale love; unlike first loves, last loves were usually tricky to identify simply because hope, blind as fuck, goes on waiting and hoping and praying and wishing till the very end, fingers crossed, legs uncrossed. But his time was up, and he knew this in a contented, satiated way.

He liked the liquid identity of his new love, the face now woman, now man, so in sync with the universe. Gods and genies are assigned gender by men...That glow on the birdie-birl's face last night, the milk of human kindness in its breast! He had met with an angel, that's who.

He was happy, happy, happy. Most of all he was happy his new love had left him mid-love so he could for the first time in his life love on and on. Some may call it too late but to him it was a dream come true not a moment too soon.

To be loved was magic enough, but to love was to turn the wand on oneself.

~

Her expression as she ended the story was serene. (She could look ethereal or eerie depending on the light). I was loath to pull her out of the fairy tale she'd spun around herself snug as a spider web but this time I did have a question. 'Were you the...birl?'

She adjusted her voluminous skirt and said, no, not at all.

The stories were strangenesses. Rumours of a world I was yet to enter, a world up and running. My whole body a well in the wilderness into which she gibberished, waiting for echoes, for it all to make sense back to her. Till today I do wonder if the stories were fact or fiction, or a cunning mix of the two. What she said, what she didn't, buried like half-seeds in the soil of my skin. Jack-in-the-box words. Creeping up behind me on silent feet of butter to cup my eyes—*who am I*?

3

IT OCCURRED TO me that her husband must have been years and years older than her if she could look back on his death as an old man—maybe an arranged match with material benefits. For the record there was no job she was known to have held or parental property she mentioned having inherited; so where did this unending prosperity come from?

People often tried to piece together the chronology of her husband's adultery. My own mother had looked defeated once. 'How many women can a man manage in one lifetime?'

As many as there are stars in the sky, yielded Nena's secret math.

She caught me loitering with my hands behind my back during the day, and put up that eyebrow much like a child would a tongue. Quick to mock my brooding. 'Moping around is what *I* do, this is my house to mope around in. You come here...what *do* you come here for?'

I shrugged. Neither my mother nor I had any clear idea why I was here, we only hoped Nena one day would.

She disappeared into her bedroom and returned with—I looked again—a lute?

'Play,' she bade sweetly.

I plucked a string, making it amply clear I'd never met a music instrument before.

'I can see the future,' she said matter-of-factly and took the lute back. I wandered a little as she fiddled with it. Past the veranda to where ginger gnarled the soil, mud glandular from empty mansions left behind by millionaire earthworms...I took a deep breath and stretched myself, knowing myself to be absolutely alone. Closing eyes was a luxury; always I felt the need to see who saw me. That was when I heard her play.

I don't know, really I don't, if I learnt my way around a guitar by my mid-thirties because I thought she foresaw a vision of me thus, or if she meant that her story about the geriatric husband was of him somewhere down the line as a ripe old fool of hundred. All I know is that when her fingers began to strum, a place fit for angels descended on us.

I went back in and she never glanced up once, thankfully missing the unbecoming laxity to my jaw. The sparking of fingers, the rapt transported air. Eyes closed, chin slanted, hair side-parted so deep it hid her cheek to chin...Like earth poised for spinning.

'Beware of those like me,' she said with an apologetic smile, tossing one end of her fringed shawl over a bony shoulder, 'who think themselves talented.'

But you must play to audiences, to…to crowds, I stuttered.

She saw me to the gate holding an umbrella over us—it was neither sunny nor raining. 'Shall we run away together?' she asked politely.

I'd be glad to, I assured her, for my mother was driving me bats. I wanted to get out, out of my house, my corner of the world, my skin.

~

If I thought my mother would protest or raise objections, I was way off the mark. She had already applied for my passport and borrowed from her closest kin warm clothes for me to carry just in case. The thought of me in another country tickled her, and she giggled into her palm as she buzzed around the house organising my exit.

Gratified perhaps by this blind trust we placed in her, Nena relented a little. 'Women travelling alone look suspicious. But I need you for far more than ornamental purposes. You see,' she paused, burying a bobby pin deep in her bun. 'You see…' Again, she paused.

'I just want to thank you,' I said more emotionally than I would have liked.

She waved a hand, dismissing my lower-class gush. 'I am not perfect,' she started again. 'My parents brought me up...they did not really bring me up, I brought myself up. I did what I wanted, climb trees, run around with friends, collect books...How much I read! I read till my eyes turned in their sockets and I was looking into my own eyes! My mother never learnt to read, you see, her parents distrusted alphabets more than anything. It was a power that can destroy, they said about reading, about learning. Only boys know what to do with knowledge. They kept my mother simple and, in their eyes, young forever. But dispositions sour anyway, books just take the fall...

'Someday I will tell you about all the books I possessed, I never gave a single one away. I read them again and again, I knew them by-heart. My parents never gave me their house, they willed it to their son, my brother, who, I later heard, just gathered up my books and dumped them in the river! When I heard this I was too numb to cry. I am still too numb to cry. They were my childhood companions, I fought with them, I made up with them, they are what I call my mind, they are this conversation I'm having. One day I will jump into that river.'

I cleared my throat. Fascinating though this digression about her private library was, we were to travel soon and there were related issues to be aired. Little did I know then that those books at the bottom of an unknown water body would figure in our travels.

In a small voice she returned to what it was she set out to say. 'I was telling you that I was never trained for...' she whispered the next word. I was expecting 'life' but surely I didn't just hear 'men'?

I nodded, dying to ask her to repeat that last word I'd heard wrong.

'So, you see, I never...'

Again I nodded, more to alleviate her palpable discomfort.

She then said briskly, 'So this is what I must do. I have made a list of all my husband's infidelities. We revisit the place, the spot, locate the people and find out if this was true or a figment of my imagination. You understand? I want to clear my name in my head. Am I just another common suspicious wife? I couldn't bear that! I need to know. Or how else will I calm down enough to die anytime soon? Am I wronging *Someone* or is *Someone* laughing his head off so much his head is never on?'

I'm not, she said mock-collaring me, hysterical. 'Hysteria means a wandering uterus. Gypsies wander, so do bards—which uterus has been stopped at a toll gate?'

~

We sat facing each other in a train bustling up north, our backs upright, hands primly on knees. The journey would take two days and one night. The coach first class and we the only occupants; few could afford a luxury such as this. At stations people jumped out and stretched themselves on platforms. We watched them avidly then, as we did those who waited for other trains to come and whisk them away to other places. We ate what we got from the train pantry, which came in hot aluminum foils with toy spoons. (My only rail journey, made last year when an uncle dropped me off at my college, was the opposite of this. I travelled sitting up the whole way and ate what my mother packed, food that spoilt in the heat by evening. When I stole away from college, I sat in the back of lorries and starved all the way back.)

A water pouch spilt and she shrank into her berth, not putting a foot down till it was mopped, had completely evaporated. She was a performing artist, I reminded myself, still asking as expected of me, 'What about the nine months in amniotic fluid? If you're so allergic to water?'

'My mother thought she'd delivered a pineapple. My epidermis came from Hell. So unprepossessing an infant was I that no portrait was commissioned. Bath times were particularly barbaric with my deafening wails, so this was delegated to maids, who didn't care about my cleanliness one way or another and left me alone at first cry. The real war started at puberty. Until then I was thought to be someone with nightmare skin—oh, the magic oils my father splurged on! I still took liquids those days even though my throat closed up for hours afterwards. And then like all children do I ran away from home one day. The skies split with a roar, the downpour the last thing I remember. After I was found prostrate off an over-bridge by a search party, the doctors noticed the pattern of rain on my skin. It ran like a river of fire over me, in blisters and sores. While I waited for new skin to grow, this is what I learnt—water takes a matchstick to me.

'By now I've designed my own annual bath. Baste petroleum jelly, cool water in a bucket and pour over head in one swoop, without delay wrap up like a mummy in layers of cotton and breathe out hard to expel moisture from the nose...Seventy percent of earth is water, seventy percent of us is water—what can I say, I'm allergic to me.'

I blinked in disbelief. No one I knew washed once a year.

'Do I tell you too much?' she asked solicitously.

I shook my head.

She too shook her head. 'I have to grow you, else I will have no one to know me.'

~

Next evening we took adjacent rooms in a comfortable resort and quickly met up for dinner. It was late and we were tired. I had started to worry she had no plan for the next day but she set me right over dessert. And she did it in her usual bald way.

'Let me tell you about the first time I should have suspected *Someone* but didn't. Much, much later, when I brought this up, along with all the other "incidents of stress" as I call them, he laughed right in my face. He laughed so much! Every time I accused him of being with another woman he laughed. And you know what? I'd laugh right back and that would be that.'

Addicted as I was to her tales, this time I felt a shift in tone. Like blade met bone. It was there in the way she fidgeted on her chair (usually she owned what she sat on—I'd seen her since in planes and trams and cycle-rickshaws, and they just looked like feet or wings, simply the rest of her). Maybe I was expected to lean forward and squeeze her hands lying silent in her lap. But when she spoke, she sounded just as she always did—like a boatman rowing over calm waters.

~

Newly married but he felt no different. The dowry was being transferred to his debtors, to his business; it would pay backdated salaries of all his staff and servants, settle all the lawsuits. The world could eat his shit! He looked sideways at his bride. Eighteen and untouched. He knew all the signs. At a premarital outing when his hand brushed hers, she had jumped out of her skin.

On the wedding night her umpteen blushing cousins swam him through a sea of candles. His bride of—he did a quick count—eight hours sat with her legs tucked under her. There were socks on her feet. Socks! School-girl despite superhuman efforts to present her as a gazelle in gauze—between them, him the adult at thirty-four.

'What would you like to do?' Without meaning to his voice oozed none of the syrup it usually did when he approached the opposite sex. Intuitively he knew she must never have the upper hand. This was no roll in the hay; this was lifelong combat.

'Can you tell me a story? I'm in the mood for one.' Hands steepled under chin, plaits thick jute jutting off her head. Such smug bridal specialness! He felt the bile rise in him, it always did when he came across people who never had to go hungry or wait in queues for handouts.

He had a choice in that split second; he could fake a jocular uncle aura or he could be a tycoon, someone who owned her, the CEO of her soul. He thought of her father, a cut-throat businessman who had come up the hard way by betraying every partner he did trade with; he thought of her mother, cowering and subdued, laughing when her husband laughed, frowning when her husband frowned. Unnaturally attached to him, as if he was above the almighty. Whom had this girl taken after? He did not make the mistake of looking at her; she may take it as some kind of power over him. As it is, her flawless diction, pedantic literary references and blind faith in the goodness of mankind struck terror in his heart. All that he cooked up—the high status of his late family, the rich heritage of land and a careless prosperity—served her parents right. They should have been more vigilant. So keen had they been to get their only daughter married to him. Him!

Without acknowledging his bride he turned around, lay on the jasmine-strewn bed and slept soundly. The next day, without a word to her, he set out for the city of his work. He would come back for her, he told her father, by and by. With this, he was sure, he had put her in her place. Her and her picture-book family.

The bride sat dreamily by the river beside her house, her sole grouse that she did not feel married yet. Instead, she felt light, too light, light as the breeze cartwheeling around her. Everything seemed doable; it had all been done before, would keep being done. She reaffirmed the resolve to herself—I will have a happy marriage. Happy.

Six months later this resolve felt a little premature. He had neither come back nor sent for her. Unknown to her, her father had sent word to her husband but the latter pleaded delay in the setting up of the marital homestead. It was true that their wedding had taken place rather quickly, but that was more because the groom needed capital for a brilliant new venture and could not wait. Her own plea that she was too young had fallen on deaf ears. Her parents said she was ripe for marriage, for setting up her own home. It sounded tempting to her suddenly, this notion that she could be her own person. She'd paint her walls chameleon, read through the night, flood friends with the finest of gifts, and how much she would make herself laugh...She had nodded then; yes, I will marry, father and mother, just give me a groom.

Her best friend, an orphan infamous for her runaway tendencies, came visiting from the nearby convent. She just hitched up her skirts and climbed over the convent wall at will, and each time the nuns pretended not to notice her absence, hoping she wouldn't return.

The bride welcomed her renegade friend with open arms. Much chatting ensued, most of the ribaldry sailing over her head. During the nocturnal hours that they were up discussing all things, she was convinced by her friend that she should surprise her husband in the city. Just turn up there and be ravished on the doorstep!

Pampered by family and friends, spoilt silly by minions and romance novels, any common sense by now cotton candy, she was convinced that her husband pined for her because she pined for him. Vague on exact details of consummation, she expected it to be a pleasant diversion from reading.

She told her parents she planned to shop in the city with her friend; nothing pleased them more than she frittering away her time and their money on what they called Good Taste. That was the only thing that made them shudder delicately cocooned in their chandeliered mansion—the bad taste of others. Oh, the slobber of it!

The two young co-conspirators said that after the exhausting purchasing, they would spend the night at a family friend's place. Later, of course, she would tell her parents all. Right now, it was to be a surprise. She didn't want them, in a parental fit, to alert her husband to her impromptu arrival. This was a perk of being married after all, that one got to do things on one's own at last.

It was a dishevelled-looking pin-code. The friend, who was meant to vanish after dropping her at her husband's bachelor digs, shifted from one foot to the other as the puzzled guard told them that the master had not been here in a long time and who exactly did they say they were? They waited an hour or two and, after ardent enquiries, reached the area of his work. He wasn't there either. Leaving word there they returned to his empty address and settled down on a bench nearby to wait.

No suspicion smote her soul. She only waited to see the dazzle in her husband's eye when he saw her, this moment that they would talk about fondly throughout their wedded bliss, to dinner guests, to the grandchild they dandled on their knee; it would be part of their togetherness lore...

The friend was beginning to look frazzled and a pitying glint had entered her eye when it rested on the girl. The guard had told her slyly that the master could be at a not-nice area in the outskirts. Oblivious, the girl only waited for who she had started to call in her heart of hearts, Beloved.

A terrible cawing woke her up from an impromptu nap on the stone bench. No crows, just Beloved and his ear-splitting fury. For a blind upward sweep of the second it took her eyelashes to part she experienced pure joy. Then she realised she was being scolded. For the first time ever. In public. In no uncertain terms. In language most foul. From a mouth palsied by its contents. Of course, even as he vented his ire, she forgave him. She saw it coming from a concerned space, from fears for her. Those days she was habituated to everything being about her.

She waited for his eyes to halt at her face, on her eyes. But no. No welcome, no missing of her, neither food offered nor beverage. Just this rambling rationale of whereabouts the previous night. She fidgeted impatiently through the torrent of words, intense and jabbing. How he went to visit a childhood friend of his late mother, who lived alone and afraid far away from here, so that he went there from time to time whenever he could, to enquire after her, help her in whatever way he could. 'An elderly woman!' he said. An old aunt, an old maid, jumping at every sound, nervy, suffering from indigestion and heartburn. Of unsound mind and a thousand wrinkles. Rags of bedding held down by calcified bones.

She understood his charity, his benevolence, his pure heart that came to him via the right values instilled during childhood, while she...did have a different upbringing and how how how could she not agree with this man she was going to love till she lived, that he was, in fact, made of a goodness superior to hers?

He made no attempt to appease her or even entertain her, curtly ordering her back to where she came from, saying he had too many crisis meetings to attend and that he would send for her when the house was ready, hadn't he told her that, *hadn't he*? Since he trembled unbridled in high temper while asking her this, there was only one answer. Yes, she had been told. Yes, she knew.

She looked at him, the man she would honeymoon a lifetime with. His cheeks, his chin, his chest...all a burnished blur. That was the first thing she had noticed about him, the ripple of his skin even when he wasn't moving, as if he was made of impatient muscles. His beauty was the wild kind, waiting, she sensed, to be unleashed upon her. And though she shied away from the graphic images her friend had hinted at, she did think she would soon be divided into two, that indeed all women were divided into two—a young girl doted on by parents and a young woman in her husband's hot embrace. And look at him! From the overlong hair kissing his shoulders to the boots of leather that she could not take her eyes off when he sat with his legs crossed, he was like all the heroes of all her books come alive.

She accepted her error, apologised for her impertinence, and prepared to travel back chastened. She felt mature, like she was finally a grown-up. This is what life is as an adult, she told herself. Making mistakes and owning up. Husbands and wives spend a lifetime together, what is a year or two apart? When they did start to live together it would be such a firework in the sky. For now she likened herself to a mermaid who had to leave the sea and adapt to... diesel-fumed highways.

Good girls from good families would never do what she just did. He rolled his eyes meaningfully at the friend, the one whom all fingers now pointed at, so that she herself could remain spotless, without blemish—it was only the company she kept. His eyes and his hands, the angle of his chin, the flaring of nostrils, all of it conveyed undiluted shock at the scandal of her turning up like this, and he had to abandon pressing professional errands to run around ensuring her safe journey back. Eyes downcast, she thanked him for everything. Every.

Neither friend spoke on the return journey, lichen from the stone bench had found its way to their tongue. The giddy-headed giggles of the onward journey were ripples of shame in their bloodstream.

The girl felt drained. Marriage had suddenly broken her spirit, she could glimpse heartbreaks ahead. Her eyes were damp, her body soggy with this prescient knowing. Love had been broken down to her as a duty to be performed—not an emotion to be felt—and it drenched her from inside out, like a rain rained wrong.

~

'My friend told me in parting the name of that place, where my husband had been. In fact, she kept repeating it as if it should mean something to me. And I did remember it all these years. These no-man strips between two states left alone by rulers on either side. Where anything goes. I hope to find it today.'

In the brightly lit dining area, her voice came to a halt. We moved towards the stairway. She stopped two steps above me. 'I knew straight off he did not trust women, but I thought, as all arrogant brides do, I would be the one to change all that, that he would trust me and so trust all women. But this is what happened, I didn't trust him, so now I don't trust any man.'

Her words entered me, like all her words did, in the manner of a blood transfusion, smooth as truth, like I had said them myself. The yeast of her voice lent the parables their leavening, that swell of tasty air. Her voice—part-goosebump, part-prophecy—she culled from deep within her, changing atmospheres, changing the very air. Sometimes I could smell what she said she did, see who she said she saw. Her brow spat up a vein, face shuffled features. I couldn't face that face. It would have been too much, to hear her *and* to see her.

In my room I lingered in the washroom, never once glancing at the smudged mirror on the wall; no one in the glass to look at if you ask me. Stretched out on a lumpy mattress, my head floated now and then like a balloon off a string and my feet wobbled as if a railway track still ran under them. I watched what I thought though—the night was listening.

~

She did not look calm or collected the next morning. 'I slept poorly,' she kept saying, but it was more than that. She was on edge. She rummaged through the steel trunk and found what she was looking for in a cloth-bag hanging off her bedpost—the brass lamp from home. Neither lit it nor rubbed it. Why wake a genie? Let's go, she sighed, taking off her glasses. This trip had cost her some unmasking; the glasses were part of that.

'I want to check the address he mentioned, where that poor elderly spinster lived alone with only my husband occasionally for protection at night. He was over thirty then, his mother the same age as I was when he was born, this woman her childhood friend. If I was sixteen years younger than him, she was sixteen years older.'

A tremor ran through her. But her voice was fine when she directed the taxi driver, who was voluble on the area we were going to. 'Parts of it have been renovated, so the address you are looking for may not be there any more...'

'It is my old domestic help,' she told him, winking amiably at me. 'I must find her. I had a dream that she was ill.'

The cabbie told us in great detail about his own dreams, every single one he ever dreamt from the time he first dreamt, or so it seemed to me, listening to his monotone. I saw urchins sleeping on pavements, second-hand books heaped up on kerbs, shop shutters half-open, peanuts being boiled, corn on coal gone cold.

When we got out of the cab, she clutched my elbow (the rest of me twitching to keep every bit of that elbow still). There was an assortment of shabby buildings in row after row of infectious penury. I walked with her, humouring her need for nostalgia, for closure. Her breath had turned to pant though we were taking the shortest of strides. I was not curious about her yet though—that would come much later. Right now I was letting her...happen.

'I feel more lost today than I did then,' she said.

I stayed silent. The new trousers my mother had stitched for this trip scratched my legs with nails of wool. The weather was warmer than two of our hottest summers back home put together. I was beginning to feel a little foolish. Who wouldn't? No compass, no map, only hunches. My companion more and more like one of those women who speak to themselves on street corners...

I jolted to a stop—she wasn't by my side. I looked back, and there she was, peering down a mud track. I obediently followed her into the lane.

'Here,' she said, pointing unsurely.

I sauntered into a tea-stall opposite. 'We are officials from a government charity that rebuilds homes for people below the poverty line. Can you help us see one of these houses, for us to gauge measurements and requirements etc and then draw up a feasible budget?'

The man, pouring tea from one tin can into another so that it frothed up, swept his eyes over Nena, a wraith hovering in the sunlight, a hand to her temple, looking anxiously about. She looked like she was searching for more than an address, her eyes scurrying mice-like all over the neighbourhood.

He told us he would help us, as he, like the rest of the people in this hell-hole, had tired of not having enough to eat or a roof to sleep under, and the mountains of tax they had to pay and pay even after they died. I smiled weakly under the onslaught of such hot young angst, hoping I looked well on my way to fixing the world's woes.

In such fraudulent manner did we enter one of those parodies of home. A basic room with an open lavatory in the corner, it took all sixty seconds of a minute to go over the place.

'He stayed here on what should have been my honeymoon, with a woman unrelated to him by blood. He did that for her, a strange woman, out of the goodness of his heart, expecting nothing in return, and me, his wife, he sent away with a sweet nothing.'

I gave no indication I was listening. I felt incredibly lofty; she should have known, was my smug aside.

'When I mentioned this to him on a wedding anniversary, he said, don't tell me you were jealous of an old hag! When what he should have said was, oh, how I wish I had gathered you in my arms and kissed you all day that day.'

She shook out some pills from a handkerchief in her voluminous pocket, dry-swallowed them and faced me squarely, challenging me to voice my opinion. I said nothing, she had heard herself speak. I was sure that was the first time she put it to herself like that, in so linear a fashion.

But she wasn't going to let me get away scot-free. 'This had to be carnal, right? I am correct, you agree, in thinking he knows this woman in the Biblical sense?

It is not my dirty little mind, a suspicious nature, me being typically, you know, female?'

At last, I faintly began to understand her mission. She was going to hunt them down, these ghosts in her marital bed, and haunt them right back one by one. And I was to sing for my supper, to listen and nod appreciatively. I was the jury she bribed in advance.

'Yes, Nena,' I said. 'He was fucking this woman.'

For the first time in that long pointless day her lips lifted in a smile. Shoulders slumped in their usual arc—she had been holding them stiffly since morning—she said, as if all of language was one word, 'Thanks.'

~

The next morning at the airport she was dressed truer to her new character; narrow legs encased in fitted blue denim, feet in white canvas shoes, a full-sleeved white shirt tucked into the waistband. She looked exactly who she was; a tourist exploring life so far, the dim-lit corners of long ago.

Years on I have studied many women at airports dressed in smart casuals, biting lip, mentally going over the next course of action, their journey just begun but imbued with a sure knowledge of being on the right path, however messy.

She turned to me when they announced our flight and said gravely in Gujarati, '*Jevu dekhai evu hotu nathi*. Nothing is as it seems. But sometimes everything is exactly how it looks.'

Women of ill repute, the shopkeeper had called them, the original occupants of those illegal plots. She repeated the words 'women of ill repute' on a note of worship.

4

MY FIRST TIME in air was marred by heavy vomiting. Barely had the plane started to paw the ground like a great mythical beast taking off for an inter-galactic war when my stomach turned upside down. Everything I ever ate reached my mouth in a single leap.

As my insides evacuated into paper bags, provided with commendable punctuality by the heavily made-up air hostesses in their identical shapeless silks, Nena nimbly moved out of the way. I was beyond embarrassment, convinced I was dying, dramatically missing my mother, even my father. Nena had given me the aisle seat in view of my unbending bamboo limbs. When she unbuckled my seatbelt after takeoff, I almost tumbled into the aisle demanding that God take me then and there, that very moment. In reality I just sat there like a paralytic and blew a spit bubble.

With one empty seat between us she spooned me some soup and made me sip water with gloves on. Oh, yeah, her so-called hypersensitivity to liquids, was my last thought before I fainted or slept, wanting only to wake up in the Other World, in God's kingdom or at least God's kitchen garden.

Back on land where my vital organs stopped trying to swap places, I sheepishly regretted missing out on a story. Clouds chasing after us, bodies suspended mid-air...perfect setting for that voice of hers.

We were in an acquaintance's empty house by late afternoon, stocking up on food as if for a siege. After I bathed and she didn't, we settled in a stranger's home, on a stranger's sofa, and drew up our next shaky strategy.

~

By the time she joined her husband in the city—with the blessings of her parents, which just meant ferrying as many pots and pans possible, three servants and other house-warming gifts expected from the girl's side—she was raring to go, to start her happy marriage.

One of the new servants gave into her safekeeping a bit of money, saying, please give this to me if I ever ask.

'What is this for?' barked her newly minted mistress.

'Madam, my mother gave this to me out of her savings. She said if anything happens to you there, so far away, just have enough to pay your way back home by any means you can.'

'Anything happens to you here!' The mistress could only laugh at such servant-class phobias and fears. Her own mother had cheerily waved. No one expected her back.

It didn't occur to her that perhaps all brides should have a bit of personal dowry sewn into their hems thus, an exit route provided by those who send them away. After all, men went to fight wars carrying swords, women were sent out into the world with silly smiles and synonyms for 'sorry'. She did have an aunt who came back home the very next morning after her wedding. Guests were still sleeping off the moonshine and when they came to, the bride of the previous day was sitting among them like she never left. No one asked her what happened. She just never returned to her husband, that's all, and lived in her father's house till he died and then in her brother's house till she died. A lady of such tranquil disposition and translucent skin that everyone presumed the bridegroom had done something unspeakable to her.

But absconding brides were not on this girl's radar; she was hell-bent on being happy, absolutely rabid about it. To that end, she could throw feasts and festivities in a jiffy, banter in cultured accents, wrap herself in tinsel when the occasion demanded. People of all vintage and class, those who took favours from them and those they took favours from, everyone was enchanted by this chit of a girl, the recent little bride of Mr So and So.

The husband, who had given her nil encouragement when she landed up, now began to see the brighter side of wives. She was someone he spoke of highly in public; it didn't matter that they had separate bedrooms in separate wings. She, a nebulous haze at the tail-end of his vision most mornings, was his respectability, the capital that recast his fortunes. She made him look good, that's what trophy wives did.

She still caught her breath when he walked by. To her utter and everlasting shame, when he trailed a finger down her bare arm after dinner as they tried to locate the full moon from her bedroom balcony one night, she had scooted away without any noticeable grace. It had been instinctive. She had also—she tried never to remember this—made a funny illiterate sound deep in her throat, like a hunted animal that got its foot out of a snare in time.

Thankfully, he seemed to have forgotten the incident by breakfast the next day, where she met him with the same wifely concern she had unfailingly evinced from day one. She served him his breakfast and gave him piping hot tea. She smiled and made small talk till her throat hurt. He treated her with his customary indifference, cutting into her chatter with unrelated instructions. When he left she collapsed in her bed. Why was she not a seductress like those seductresses in the books she read in secret? Those fluttery women whose exposed backs are kissed by men.

She got up and took out the satin slip from her trousseau trunk. She shook it open and held it against her, letting the fabric flow to her knees. She moved towards the mirror on dainty tiptoe, swaying her hips like she imagined a femme fatale would. The woman in the mirror with tilted chin and puffed mouth was too ridiculous to be borne; falling to the floor in giggle fits, she forgot all about her husband.

She thought then they had all the time in the world. That one fine day he would take off his daily everyday 'husband' mask and turn to her ardently with 'now, tell me everything about you'. That day he would fall irrevocably in love with her because everyone always loved her forever. And then. And then all the other mysterious stuff would follow—what books said happened only in beds.

For now she knew that she would always, always shiver at the first sight of moon at night, with its oily practiced stillness and simple round face.

~

During one of his many travels away from home, she was invited to a beautiful party, a party everyone was going to. Her husband would have wanted her to go, she told herself, and wrapped herself in tinsel yet again. She liked that ordinary people seemed to light up when she spoke to them. Her kindness she exercised like a weapon. It gave her the luxury of actually doing nothing; she only watched as whole adults unspooled just because she listened, murmured softly, paid attention. Lovely to meet you, they said; lovely to be met, she said. An admirer once told her, 'You have such an open way of meeting eyes.'

She arrived fashionably late at the party, and joined a group of men who fell silent as she approached. She soon had them all roaring with laughter, and was about to move away when one of the men, someone who worked with her husband, turned towards her in such a way that the rest of the group was excluded.

'And, my dear, how do you find marriage to be?'

She laughed delightedly. With a light hand on his arm, she leaned in to confide, 'Like I am a farmer growing rapture on my land.'

For a split second, just before the man laughed back, she spied a look. With spite in it and malice.

'What is it?' A shot in the dark, but disconcerting how quickly her tone changed to a tight knot. The man before her felt as if his neck was in a noose, as if he had to tell her everything he knew or bleed from the nose.

He just about managed to scoff, as if joking, 'Tell that husband of yours to behave more married, that's all.' And Nena smiled stiffly, aware of his misstep.

Discreet enquiries soon yielded results. A love triangle; two business partners and the woman who ran the staff kitchen. Her husband, she was told in measured whispers, one of the two suitors.

She almost laughed. How clichéd! How entirely expected! She could forgive anything but doing the done. A rival of stunning looks, of legendary wit, of such enormous reading that each word of hers a book in itself, she could just about take—but this? Sounded paltry, like armed robbers making off with an empty jewellery case, leaving the necklace behind.

Those were the days women seldom worked. If they did, they were considered fair game. In connected matters, like elopement or a love child, there would be no support ever—not social, not legal, not familial. The woman was said to have won only if she could manage to convince her paramour to leave everything and everyone he knew behind and set up home with her in exile, and then too she would have to watch him with bated breath for signs of further straying. What the other woman fears most is other women; having won a man with wiles, male idiocy is a scientific fact to her.

After that party her thoughts grew noisy, pebbles in a tin dragged on rocks. It was not like she feared being left, or neglected, or done out of her share of real estate. The house she lived in was huge, filled with the prettiest of things, and belonged entirely to her, deeds and all. Her father had stipulated that much, since it was made with his money and came to her in dowry. Any husband who shared it with her, incidental.

She had no clear idea what to do with the

information that had fallen into her lap; in her heart she could not believe it. The way she saw it, she was an unparalleled beauty (too many people said this to her with annoying regularity), had a head jam-packed with wisdom (she knew what anyone was going to say long before they did and it took all her effort to patiently wait for them to find their fullstops), and, well, she had this house, didn't she? She thought, she really did, that fidelity to her was a cakewalk.

So she waited up for her business-touring husband night after night till he came back home at last, sooty in lung from travel. He used to say there was dust even in his gut at the end of these long journeys through dirt tracks and shortcuts. She would serve him cool liquor in tall glasses, with nuts and dates in her whitest china. But this time she barely let him past the marbled lobby. As if reading out a prologue from a classic, she told him in tones suitably sepulchral of his alleged trespass. (A kind of detached curiosity was upon her. Let's find out, she thought, could any man be that foolish, so blindingly trusting in lust?)

His tenderness evaporated, his indulgent manner replaced with uproar. He first mourned her mistrust in him, then berated her loudly for suspecting him like only bad wives do; he never wanted to see her face again.

Nonplussed by this counter-attack, where she expected amused denial or even a grovelling at her feet, she said, 'Word is you offered marriage.' This was a calculated lie, but the bucket she threw blindly into the well came away sloshing water.

His voice changed to rich injury. 'This is a rumour put about by my former business partner to undermine me in my own space. The jealous viper! Ever since my capital came into the business, he's been insecure. But this!'

A twist in the story had just occurred, and she respectfully heard him out. It must be added that she willingly met her husband halfway at all such junctures that were to dog their married life. Turning a blind eye, as some may term the situation, was just attention deficiency on her part. She knew that demanding explanations from him—where were you? with whom?—would mean a spectacular show of like and loyalty from her in return. And while in her fantasies she was the perfect spouse, she was aware that wifely duties perhaps extended beyond housekeeping, and she did not want to get into any of that. One day perhaps...

She did have moments of doubt, who wouldn't? Earth had always sugar-coated itself when it saw her approach. Now dense undergrowth tangled up her feet. Fangs sank into her neck out of nowhere. She wanted to lick the world and find it confectionary again.

To her credit she even tried out the following words—'Let's go our own ways.' She said them only to see how they'd taste in her mouth. No woman left her husband, only husbands left wives. But when she did address them to her husband all hell broke loose within him.

First he howled, werewolf in a fable. He then gripped the window grill hard and wept. 'Don't leave me,' he cried, appearing to toss pride aside. *Ne ma quitte pas,* she translated dreamily. Always the main protagonist in her own tale, she felt as if his tears dried on her cheeks. Her heart melted, a puddle under her bodice. As she faced him that day, she took the decision to believe him, to maintain status quo, to keep the walls of her own world vertical. Reading fiction had never come in this handy before.

All rumours about him died a natural death; nothing but paper, kites that flew too high. If the wife trusted him, the world trusted him. The business partner slunk away to the suburbs tail between his legs and her husband won the day. She was stupid enough to think it was she who won the day.

~

'What did he do all day, you ask,' she said, though I asked no such thing and never would have. 'Overlord of the underworld. His job, from what I could make out, was to approach you and offer not to kill you if you paid more than your enemy just did to have you killed. Of course, he did a lot of research, finding out about your enemy and probably even provoking your enemy into making that offer that he then provides a counter-offer for. But more often than not just a trick for you to fall for and pay him to maintain your good name or your life, whichever happened to be under threat. And once in a while someone did get killed.'

I blinked. I knew she thrived on my disbelief, so I muted my reaction to 'a boring conman then'.

A small pause before she agreed. 'Boring.'

Out came the lamp. She studied it long, much like astronomers pore over a supernova. She said without looking at me, 'I do this to make my wishes clearer to me, not some genie.'

I nodded my head. My silence, she had said before, kept her on her toes.

5

COME MORNING, WE were stealthily staking out a sprawling residential building called—let me remember this right—Tarana. Could mean melody, could be apartment owner's late daughter's name, said Nena. The guard surveyed us snootily, surely underpaid for the ruckus he was prepared to raise with unannounced visitors, like this was a maximum-security jail and we mere pickpockets. He went up the stairs to inform our quarry of our arrival.

Soon the very man we wanted to meet appeared on his balcony, hands on hips, chin way up, straining at us with eyelids so low on his eyes he looked fast asleep. Nena waved in a friendly manner, then she signalled to him languidly, inviting him down, as if where we stood was a vast meadow with swaying grass and not a cramped parking lot with broken flowerpots and stray dogs. He vanished from sight only to reappear at a window, as if we were hallucinations he may not see from another angle.

The guard laboured down those steps and informed us that the gentleman would have no visitors today. Can we come tomorrow, we asked. No, he said. The day after? No. Then when?

'Listen,' he said, seriously doubting our ability to take a hint. 'Sir is not there.'

What do you mean, we spluttered. We just saw him at his balcony and at his window, and Nena was dead sure it was him though she was not wearing her glasses and his sideburns were dyed an improbable black.

The guard tapped his head. 'He is not in here.'

Ah, insanity, such a neat summing-up of all of humanity. I asked if he would take up a little note from us, for which we would pay hard cash. He said he would do this only because his heart was big and his soul so white and that money was evil but his children too many, so we paid him all the small change we had between us, and sent up this note:

'Where is she who you fought my husband for?'

In some time, panting and sweating profusely, he brought down a note that read thus: 'I didn't fight your husband. He fought me.'

As we prepared to pen our next missive, the guard put a hand to his heart. With his other hand he indicated we could go up ourselves. Before he changed his mind, we ran up the spiral stairway, taking two steps at a time, and pressed the concerned doorbell with an unrelenting finger. But the reclusive householder inside kept his door tightly shut as if he had died after spotting us.

Nena banged on the door and frantically twisted the knob like she'd been locked out of her own apartment. From within came his high-pitched shout eventually. 'I lost everything. My wife left me, no one would give me a job...'

Nena pretended not to hear him, saying 'Eh? Eh?' gormlessly, provoking him into louder, angrier words that lost all nuance at that speed and scale.

'Rehana,' he said in soprano, opening and shutting the door. A quick glimpse of scotch-taped spectacles, an old vest spliced open to the navel.

'Where is Rehana right this minute?'

'Rehana is my wife.' Again the door opened and shut.

'What about the woman not Rehana, the woman not your wife?'

There was the sound of retreating footsteps. We felt like abject failures.

'I thought we had established a rapport,' said Nena, who was used to instant fandom.

A frayed paper was thrust through the semi-open door. A love letter in unchaste Hindi which Nena roughly translated thus:

Dearest, darlingest, a piece of my own liver,

You know I love only you. Alas, however much I love and however long, no love, mine or yours, can purify me again, spoilt as I am forever from this moment on. He—with his heart as black as charcoal—took from me that one thing I kept only-only for you. As a woman I have lost all there is to lose. You live happily, that's all I ask the lord night and day.

Jaan

Jaan, I said jubilantly, we have the name. Nena still frowned at the letter, no doubt computing the number of grammatical errors in a single paragraph.

The door opened fully. 'Only I call her Jaan. She was my life, my own, my very own. Her name was not that!'

Before he could close the door again, we took advantage of his open-mouthed shock at our stupidity and quick as a flash got into the hall that lay right behind his front door. He looked a man completely eaten up by termites. If we blew hard, he'd be sawdust.

Heads tilted back we took each other in; us because he was tall, him because of ptosis.

'Where is Jaan?' asked Nena, as if Jaan was hiding in this very house. 'Where is she?'

'Not Jaan, not Jaan.' He groaned, head in hands. 'Her name was Elizabeth. Only I called her Jaan!'

'Where is Elizabeth? Where is she?' asked Nena, fixing the typo as she spoke.

'Dead,' his voice cracked and he collapsed on a stool. 'Killed herself. What else could she do? Two powerful rivals fighting for her. Both married, both professing love for her. He is a rapist, your husband, he raped my Jaan...'

'Elizabeth,' corrected I, recipient of a quick glower.

'So that's your story?' pooh-poohed Nena, wanting proper details.

'See,' he said, pointing at the threadbare sofas for us to sit, but we preferred to loom over him like playground bullies. 'This is the story of my life. I have only one life and only one story. I loved her, she loved me. We were not of the same religion, me Muslim, she Catholic. Brought up in an orphanage run by missionaries, she called herself Betty, but I told her that Betty is short for Elizabeth, and that's how she became Elizabeth. I got her a job in my company, which later became your company. Your husband—the worm, sliming his way into the apple! Suddenly he met you and came into bottomless pots of money. My poor Elizabeth was part of what he tried to snatch and make his own during that violent takeover of the business. That bit of money went to his head. He was mad with it. Mad.

'She was moved to the boss's office. She had to sit in his room for hours, pander to his whims on the menu, bring him water, bring him tea, bring him juice. Till she...don't make me say it. You want to see Jaan? Go to the St Michael church cemetery. She died on Michaelmas, the saint's feast day, September 29, so I saw to it that she was buried there. You won't catch me going there though! She doesn't live there, in that cold bit of land. She lives here.' He pointed at his chest. 'In my heart.'

We kept our eyes on his face. He was like the last leaf on a tree in the middle of autumn.

'Why did Jaan kill herself? She never meant for me to be dragged into this murkiness, for me to lose my good name. I returned to my marriage, thinking it would reduce my stress, but by Allah, that's not what marriage does!'

'I heard,' butted in Nena, 'she died in childbirth. Where will that child be now, do you know?'

'There is no child, no child,' he cried louder now, face distorted under the weight of his tragedies. 'Look!' With some struggle he took a shiny diamond ring off his little finger. 'She left me this when she died. She knew, she knew she could not go on...Her child would have been more precious to me than this! I would have brought it up like my own, any child of hers, mine.'

'Was there a post-mortem? Did they say there was no child?'

He looked stupefied. 'We buried her quick. It was a suicide! We didn't want a police case on top of everything.'

'You knew Jaan was no more?' I asked Nena, a little miffed. Why had she been trying to track down a dead woman, or was she just going with the flow?

'I'm trying to trace her family,' she replied distantly even as he yowled, 'Don't call her Jaan!'

~

We travelled back in silence. When we reached the house, she wiped her face with the end of her grey stole, and we mimed the whole tea thing we had down pat. She drained her cup into the kitchen sink and said over her shoulder, 'She must have known she was carrying, else why murder herself? She killed two people in one go.'

I sat tightly furled on the sofa, hugging my knees. Was she losing her marbles? Storyteller or mentally touched—or was that synonymous?

'If he wasn't married to me, he may have married her, she may have lived, they would be parents, there would be a child...'

She waited but I said nothing; sometimes I'm just a stray she picked off the road. After she retired for the night, I stared into the blackness outside the window. It looked deep and sweet, like slow-boiled jaggery. Daft to call nights black when none we know snow-white, twelve a.m. the colour of crow. If I remember anything from that time it was the physical weight of me, sitting or standing, walking or lying, pressing me down, down,

down into the present-tense, back to the here and now. Too young. Nena said this so often of me, it sounded like my full name, Too Young.

She had once told me, when I first began roaming her house aimlessly, that as we age memory grows stronger, that details of what happened to us long, long ago start to clarify themselves rapidly and with great urgency. This because, to please her in the beginning and to break the ice with her, I had complimented her on her unbelievable ability to reminisce in such detail. Less than a quarter her age, I was unable to revisit even a moment just gone by.

'Mind you, one starts forgetting the present by my age. I'm absent from what's happening while it is happening.'

And another day when she called me by someone else's name, she laughed. 'I only look backwards now, that's all I do. It's a wonder my head hasn't rotated front to back! In youth we have no conscience, no truck with right or wrong, we live as if we never die. And then it all returns, every word, every action, what we should have said but didn't, should have done but didn't. Till it won't let you sleep or eat. Everything you ever did was wrong. I can see it in excruciating slowness, in such vivid detail, my mistakes, the blunders that changed lives, ended lives…Why am I telling you this? You will find out soon enough on your own the truth of what I say, and it just keeps getting stronger, this knowledge that you lived your life all wrong, but it will be late, too late by then.

'I know you think you will live forever—we all do—but that's just youth's way of getting you to spend all your life as soon as you can. You pay the price at *my* age, when all you can do is hallucinate about going back in time and setting it all right and you can't—for the past is only in your head. It can be fixed only in fantasies.' Then self-jibing, 'This is what comes out of reading novels back to front. You start believing, sure, it all ended in a tragedy, but let's reverse to the beginning, to the happily-ever-before.'

Sleep swept out the rest of her words as my eyes shut of their own accord. At 1 a.m. I woke up with a crick in my neck and there peering at me as if in the middle of a conversation was she. 'I want to tell you everything, everything I know. In exchange, promise to tell me all you will know.'

Drama queen, I smile to myself even as I cross my heart and hope to die.

'That ring,' she said out of the blue as she said most things.

I looked at her politely. Not going to be dragged into her story, a story she changed one second to the next. What was it to me what she really meant, who she really meant? I was, however nicely put, the hired help. 'Paste?'

Of the purest carat. From Antwerp, geometric pinpoint centres of giant diamonds, to capture the brightest dazzle there is. Exorbitant even at cost price.

You know a lot about diamonds, I murmured, still distant, still detached.

She seemed to convulse a little, her eyes briefly white as if windows of a house high on a hill struck by lightning. She gulped down the tablets she held in her fist. 'That's my ring on his finger. I searched for it once in a mad rush. I always thought I lost it because I didn't look for it enough. When I saw it on his hand...A ring my father gave me when I was twelve, stolen by my husband for his paramour, who willed it to her one true love, who shows it off to me—to me!—today, when I am the age I am now.'

She turned to ornaments then, necklaces and eardrops and bangles and filigreed anklets gifted to her, bought for her by family and friends, for everyone knew she doted on these. I remember not a single piece of jewellery, though, only the sparkle of her speech as it caught the early morning sun. Of course she knew there had been no Jaan, the 'search' for Jaan the only known path to any family Jaan may have left behind. Now we knew for sure that her husband's dalliance with Jaan had yielded no bonny lass or lad, waiting for kindly hands to pluck it out of poverty.

Afterwards, in the peace of our joint exile, we smoked. Hookah or cigar I forget now in the comfort of my advanced age where such details blur and swirl. And the smoke that rose from our mouths like confessions we would not voice.

6

YET ANOTHER AIRPORT, this time an early a.m. though in those relentless bright lights it could well be noon. Slightly surprised to find we were headed for a city in another country, or Foreign as we call it. Nena and I were going to Foreign.

I'd been determined not to ask any questions after being misled on the previous trip about dramatis personae. Also, I had to conserve strength for all the throwing up I was going to do.

Hours and hours of whooshing about and not once embarrassing myself with projectile samples of what I ate. Hours and hours of watching Nena frown in her sleep, arguing with herself. At long last, the plane nosedived to the runway. Making our way rapidly towards the exit, propelled by an impatient crowd behind us, when she stops in her tracks and turns around. 'How did this happen? How?'

I and a million other passengers behind me crane

our necks at her. 'You a swallower of words and me with a mouth that never sleeps.' She reaches out as if intoxicated. Her hand hovers uncertainly over my head, my head hovers uncertainly under her hand. '*Lass uns miteinander sprechen, auch wenn wir keine gemeinsame Sprache haben,*' says she, refrains from patting me, and we disembark without further ado. Collect bags from the conveyor belt, straighten cramped legs. I don't ask her what she means, though she's unaware she is unintelligible to me. It is only now, in my solitude, that her meanings reach me.

All this weight I have put on in my winter years but I see myself so clearly then, stretching spine in the see-through sunshine, a sound like a long line of knuckles cracking.

~

We stayed in a neat little place near the airport, with a lobby full of coral. On different floors, so I told her we'd use her room as headquarters. She bowed low, spoke in soft Japanese. '*Anata wa issh kenmei hatarakimasu.*' 'Don't work too hard' was her favourite advice in languages I did not know when I wasn't doing a thing. All my formal references to our madcap dashing about as our own versions of legendary detectives secretly pleased her. 'This one?' she'd ask me ponderously from time to time and I'd nod gravely, usually in front of food displays. And invariably, she would pay for a loaf I had not pointed at.

I waited for a signal from her on who when what where why which how. We had ventured out of the hotel looking for quaint eateries, and even gone to an open-air art place with graffiti where despite the deep cold that could gouge your eyes out, young girls roamed in mini-skirts.

One morning she ran all the way with me at her heel...to the public library. Soon in her heaven, books for walls and floor. She posed for pictures—she lent me a creaky camera that clicked on a death rattle—with ancient book covers shaped like jewellery boxes. Look, oh, look, she exclaimed at frequent intervals. Feet in a pirouette, hands pointing, breath audible.

~

At quarter past ten Nena was down for breakfast. She looked ambushed, like everything weighed her down, even the hair on her head, especially the hair on her head. She bunched it in her fists and tugged, as if calculating its mass. Back in her room she went into the bathroom with a pair of scissors but I think it was sometime before I looked up, saw her and asked her the obvious question. Where was her hair?

'Chopped it,' she said casually enough.

I hadn't heard a thing!

'Hair's pretty silent when cut.'

The bun at the back of her head gone. I had seen her waist-length hair, more silver than white, stream behind her as she wandered around her house or while I read on that accursed sofa, the one that came to menacing life if sat upon, wheezing and blowing its nose, rearranging its innards constantly. It had been an integral part of her, that hair, now no more.

'I have more hair than you now,' I said lamely, more to say something and not stay mute in my usual awkward way.

Hmm, she said dismissively. I noticed the marmalade hoops that previously hid behind her hair. Her hair now a stubble, everything about her face reached your eye much faster. The ascetic slope of cheek, high-rise forehead, citric eyes...Like someone caught in a downpour, slicked back to skin and bone. Even her neck looked overlong though it supported a whole circus of beads.

'You are beautiful,' I said on a note of discovery and then immediately tried to retract. 'For your age.'

She did not laugh. 'You are beautiful, too, for your age,' she returned gravely.

I cleared my throat. 'Next stop?'

Walking distance, she said.

~

We went out for a late tea, not alone as I presumed. A friend of hers joined us. Tiny mincing steps, flared sleeves over elbows, pinstriped waistcoat. Loud vibrating laughs that made a tuning fork of her. Numerous squeals about not keeping in touch, what a stranger you've become, I love what you've done to your hair, that bangle is divine, mwah, mwah.

I fell off Earth straightaway. A pair of old friends meeting after a long time, the world has to scoot. So much they had to talk about, their husbands, maybe children...I wondered if Nena had kids—real ones, not the imaginary ones she was chasing.

After we had placed our orders for this tea and that coffee and some water please, Nena placed her hand over the other woman's. Nena's bony knuckles and blunt nails laced with the silver-frosted ends of Tash's dwarf fingers.

'I'm here to listen.'

At Nena's words, Tash blurted out, 'I couldn't believe it when the telephone call came from you! How did you even get our home number?'

'I knew your brother had migrated to here, and called up the embassy with your maiden name...That was the easy part.'

'So I thought, I am going to meet her. She is not here because she wants a vacation abroad, she is here to see me!'

'You have to understand, Tash, I had a baby's rattle for a head. I couldn't have handled what I knew you were trying to tell me. I couldn't have left him. Where would I have gone?'

'You were exquisite, darling. He didn't deserve you.'

'I stayed with him even after what you implied, I chose to stay with him. So I deserved him.' She adjusted some cutlery in lieu of a pause. Tash and I stared at the spoons and forks too as if it were their turn to talk. 'I have thought of you often, and am so grateful you agreed to meet me…When did you marry again?'

Tash shrugged. 'After the divorce.' She pointed at me. 'Your son? Did you remarry?'

'Oh, he,' said Nena, waving a distracted hand. Tash and I looked at her, waiting. 'He is, um, kind of a witness. You know, like, someone I can rely on to tell me later that I did this.'

'Regular or sparkling?' The waiter was back with water.

'Sparkling,' vouched my guardian.

'This?' asked Tash.

'The right thing. Doing the right thing. By you, by all I set out to meet.'

'There are others like me?' Tash's eyebrows levitated.

'I wish I could tell you, Tish-Tash, you were special. But when it comes to my husband, you are one of the crowd.'

Tash lit a cigarette. 'This is how it happened.'

~

Right, said Tash, so there were four of us in the car. The driver with my husband next to him (to keep an eye on the route, known only to him), and me in the backseat with my best friend's husband who was also my husband's best friend. There was the usual chitchat for some time, and since this was a long drive of two hours, first my husband and then I dozed off. Only when I came fully awake I knew what woke me up. My best friend's husband's finger deep where it shouldn't be.

I was disappointed. Not just because he was someone else's husband and that too yours. But also because how can he think groping without warning turns any woman on? As if sitting next to him had been foreplay enough. Where was the legendary charm, the creative persuasions that would make me override practical concerns, betray everyone? Did he think me too old, too plain, so much so that I'd jump into any male arms? Was he so used to female welcomes that he took mine for granted or was he so gauche that he didn't know how to woo?

I looked at him, and in the darkness I saw his teeth gleam white. No doubt some exorbitant dental treatment. I asked acidly, 'How's Nena?'

He laughed and made a whooping sound. 'Trust you to ask that.' He meant he wasn't fazed by my evoking your name, that it was no talisman against further attention from him. That's when I thought, I will tell Nena. She must know this. What she does with this information is not my concern, I just must tell her.

~

A small silence swallowed us whole. This wasn't a story, it was the story in a nutshell. Nena broke the tableau by coming to jittery life and reaching for her medication. 'Your water pills,' said Tash; 'I have to hydrate,' said Nena. Then she was apologising profusely, for her husband, for his arrogance, for her marriage, for her ignorance...

Tash made a face. 'Such a commonplace incident now that I think about it. But it was his conceit that did it. I've often debated about this, you know, especially in the wake of you avoiding me completely, cutting me out when I tried to get in touch. What's the right thing to do here? Is the molested to keep quiet, which the molester might take as a heads-up to molest others, or does she create a right royal stink so that the nice-guy mask comes off?'

'There are two kinds of regrets—doing what we did and not doing what we didn't. The latter somehow feels the lesser of the two,' Nena murmured. 'And wives always have this dilemma—do we kick him where it hurts or outstare the bitches acting like their husbands never did this to us! Denial is the easy way out. You have to become another person, a brand new person, a contrarian to your previous self. Also, one is never sure what is bad enough to merit a walkout. We want to be a sport, take a joke. We test our thresholds and think this is how much I can take, no, a little bit more...I did not avoid you or cut you out because I disbelieved you, but because I believed you. I wanted to postpone the decision.'

'To leave him? But...'

Shh, said Nena. 'Spies.' She had this way of expanding or shrinking me to fill whatever gap came along.

'I think spies should know,' said Tash tartly, 'what they think of fidelity and loyalty at an early age. Me, I decided long ago it was the only way to go.'

There is this old Arab tale I heard, said Nena, and Tash and I sat up.

~

An old merchant with a beautiful young wife kept her veiled and hidden deep in his fortress. The fame of her beauty spreading like incense through the land, but the sound of her laughter birdsong only to him.

Then one day the Caliph arrived when the merchant was away. The servants ran trembling to her, their mistress with the turquoise eyes—which was all they saw through her all-enveloping veil—and said that they had informed the VIP visitor of the master's absence, but he insisted he had with him a rare diamond he wanted to leave behind for the merchant to value at the earliest. Since it was the king, since it was a diamond, she made her way to her side of the door in the zenana, which is where faithful wives live of their own choice, in seclusion, among handmaids and eunuch guards. She stipulated through her slaves that she would remain hidden and put out only her hand via a small aperture in the door; the diamond could directly be placed in her hand thus, without a male eye beholding her. When the hand came out the Caliph grew giddy from its lily-whiteness, its fragrant perfection and fragility like a delicate glass sculpture come to life. All of her beauty he could compute just from that one palm stretched out before him. As he placed the diamond in her palm, he didn't know what glittered more, the stone or the hand holding it. Blood crescendoed up his ear, his retreating finger stilled to laze down her wrist for an instant, only an instant. But long enough for her to know his want, because it coiled up her spine in heady myrrh, shimmered up her collar-bones. Late the next evening the merchant was back, and she greeted him thus: 'Did you see a woman of late and crave her at first look?' All ready to launch into heated refusals when an image flashed against his will; he had indeed come across a woman with uncommon looks recently during his travels, and his eyes had rested on the tilt of her hip till he could see her no more. His wife though did not wait for his yes or for his no, she only said——when you covet a woman, a man covets me. You stray, I stray. That's the law between men and their women, remember that.

~

Though Tash snorted, arguing with its moral tone—'nothing is hunky-dory forever, not even hunky or dory'—I declared it a rather sweet story.

(I thought myself beyond ordinary mottos like fidelity and loyalty at the time, perhaps I still am and just haven't put myself to the test of late—but in that cafe in a guttural-accented country, them and I were on opposite sides of a mirror. At the time though I kept my eyes opaque, no one must look in. No one.)

They did reward my passive presence that day by letting me sample what they called nightlife. We meandered feverishly from one spot to another. I felt... no, I did not know yet what it was I was to feel. I'd incarcerated myself in a black and white world by default. I could say a thing or the opposite of it with equal conviction. 'Kill me, kill me,' shouted Time to me. In my veins blood flowed languidly downstream with paper boats in it.

Nena fashioned a turban out of her scarf to tame her 'phantom hair flying in all directions'. Often her hands went up to secure ghost hair. I was not of legal drinking age, but Nena said it was fine in these parts, that boys were made to drink early so they turn into men faster. Thus we drank and sang and confided the most bizarre things to each other and drank some more in taverns and open tents.

We need a male opinion here, they went while ordering food or deciding directions—left or right, right or left? 'Follow the man,' they told their feet. I was their lucky coin to toss, their 'heads-or-tail?' But the real connect was between them, the two friends. About people from the life they had lived together long ago. About the life they had been living right up to when they met now. Nena kept leaning forward from time to time—she sat directly in the line of breeze, always claiming the most airy spot wherever we went because 'a little sweat won't kill you guys, but for me it would mean a funeral'—with disconnected questions.

'How does sex feel, Tash? At its highest, at its best?'

'Like the very centre of you burst into giggles.'

Nena sat back as if rapped on the knuckles, her mouth a thin line. I walked out to the beach. Seemed an appropriate moment to slip out. To free them from me, to free me from them. Those days I was always eager to get away, constantly trying to leave. Like the day had a twin, twenty-four hours I hadn't lived.

I was for some reason barefoot, my toes tasting wet sand. How far I was from home, from everyone I knew; I thought how I'd lost people, addresses, even shoes, and I tried, I really tried, to feel sad. Retching, burying my face in my hands, saying sorry-sorry-sorry. Time I apologise to... Hell, I was turning into a Nena, all touchy-feely! Just the grey of the sea dyeing my soul. Giving me ideas, making me grandly begin to think I too could feel, that I was other people. I watched the rise and fall of the waves, stupid water trying to stand and falling on its ass.

I wade in.

Who salts the sea, washes water?
Who will bell the bell,
buy what I won't sell?
See eye to eye on the same face?
And whom will
my death kill?

~

When I woke up the next day, I was in bed covered with a sheet. I didn't remember the walk back or even going back to those two or none of anything at all. Nena said later that it was them who found me and that I kept insisting I had drowned. That I hugged her and wept like a baby, pointing at the sea, asking her to save me.

Sometimes Nena talks nonsense.

~

Days papered over days. We saw this, we saw that. There was drizzle, there was mist, the city in chilblains. Nena took to her bed, eyes and nose streaming. The cold, the long hours of travel, the sightseeing, the emotional reunion with an old friend, the confirmation of her husband's two-faced nature, it all finally got to her. Eyelids puffed, nostrils swollen, cheeks splotchy, red as a rose, buried under quilts. At times like this I'd remind myself of her age, her increasing frailty. Accidental exposure to water did this to her, bomb-blast her immune system. Water was the villain in her story but did this woman own an umbrella? No.

She croaked unintelligibly when I went in to ask her politely what she needed, how I could help etc. I sat next to her bed, exquisitely blank, thinking nothing, absolutely nothing. As always, time wrapped itself around me in the here and now. All my life it's been this way—this is where I start, from this instant on, wherever I am, and this is where I end. What went before, what comes after, never as painfully real as this moment to be gotten over with.

Tash, she was mumbling when I brought my ear to her fluttery lips. More to trick her into making sense, I said, 'What about her?' And what I got was coherence in return, of a kind.

'A long story. Though sometimes I've heard it in a sentence or two. Have you seen a bridge made of water?'

~

It was a boat of iron, painted black with its two ends curled up like a pantomime moustache. Flamboyantly bare. A five-year-old could lie in it with knees drawn up.

This boat—ornamental, a garden accessory, never to set sail on actual seas—was what their marriage had boiled down to. The house had been disposed of, the money divided into four shares: his, hers and their two lawyers. He wanted none of hers. She wanted none of his. Books, furniture, paintings, rugs, dog—the parting was painless. Or as painless it can be in an acrimoniously silent divorce. Because at some point they refused to talk to each other. Their lawyers, of course, charged for every syllable exchanged on their behalf. Money was anyway never the issue.

In their minds, their house—sold to the sleepy man at the back who never bid—was what kids draw with chalk on slate. One-dimensional with un-openable windows and doors in straight lines, and half a sun frozen mid-air with stiff geometric rays drawn with a scale.

The maid still got through to them, with them competing to compensate her financially for whatever ailed her. Her alcoholic husband had recently peed in the temple pond and they paid for the purification ceremony without a murmur. In fact, they had reached the police station with bail money at the same time and struggled to keep a straight face when he explained earnestly to them that it had been the lotus he had sought to use as a urinal—the pond just got in the way.

They were headed towards a fairytale divorce. Marriage, the curse of an evil fairy, a spell broken after eleven years, the long deliberations with the lawyers, the wandering in dungeons in chains, and here they were, blinking in the sudden golden sunlight, on the brink of a glossy life with mates waiting in the wings to waltz them off into the future.

Except for this black boat. That still sat in the lawn of their old home. Each had offered large sums to the other, copious tears had been shed in emotional blackmail attempts, voices had been raised and then lowered to whimpers and whispers. But the boat stayed where it was.

Seasons changed. It rained heavily, and the wind blew and blew. The boat sat through a cyclone and the hottest summer. The melt of ice creams and the hiss of squibs. There it was, always black, always solid and heavy, unmoving and alone, ensouled, in a permanent inhale.

Down the years the new owners of the house got used to seeing the estranged couple, together or separately, pottering about the boat. Cleaning it, wiping it dry, painting it a blacker black with a brush in their hands, wearing smocks reeking of turpentine.

If the new owners ever bothered to come out, they'd have seen the couple kiss the boat stern to bow and back. And heard them coo, 'Row, son, row. Row safely to the other side.'

It was a boat of iron, painted black with its two ends curled up like pantomime moustache. Flamboyantly bare. A five-year-old could lie in it with knees drawn up.

7

WE HIRED A car to the airport, and I spent the initial minutes fervently hoping I would open the window in time to puke, but instead I slept off a hangover; God, alcohol was so depressing. 'Becoming a man' such hype.

I had a friend whose father hired him a whore, and he spent his whole birthday in the lavatory refusing to come out, so terrified he'd been of manhood. Another boy I knew was taken off school for the sole purpose of manning up when his father remarried, and made to work with a carpenter, a gay carpenter who lived in the standard one-wife-two-kids home like gay men do. This boy, a friend of a friend, just went mute when no one was looking. The week he came home I had gone to visit him—this was way before my own departure for college—and he said nothing, not a word, just stared vacuously around till it was time to go back to work. It was his suicide, hushed up as an accidental death, that had the carpenter's wife scream something at the funeral, and the carpenter himself sitting there like he understood exactly what was being screamed, that set tongues wagging. Maybe being a man was just a euphemism for taking your soul in your hands and twisting its head like a rooster's.

~

We returned to India without incident, except Nena stood at an angle now, sat in a slump. Voice hoarse, skin in a rash, a look of collapse about her. She wilted on the flight back while I looked out the tiny window with exaggerated wonder. Up close the sky was anything but blue. That I could live with but where were the stars? The higher you travel, the lesser they twinkle.

Our next trip was to her birthplace.

'That domestic help I told you about,' whispered Nena when she had come awake after two full days, her voice dusty with disuse. 'Came asking for that bit of money she had given me for safekeeping, and left soon after. I knew what she was implying, that she was unhappy in my home, and I felt this huge disproportionate rage. Why couldn't she cope with real life like the rest of us? Life was like that, unpleasant and uphill.'

'*Someone* did something to this maid?' I rolled my

eyes. One thing I will say about *Someone*, he never surprises.

'It never struck me at all. Therefore, never asked her or him or anyone. It is only sitting in my home a couple of years ago that I first thought…No! Can't be! All roads keep leading to the same old, same old.'

Something clicked into place inside my head. There was a method to Nena's madness, after all. 'And now you want to find her and ask her and put yourself out of your misery. Say sorry so all's good.'

She didn't speak again till we stopped at a box-shop for refreshments (the box-shop literally a square by the roadside, with the upper plank of wood a makeshift roof and the lower side the table, locking itself up into a box when done); I had finally put her off.

'I'm a pessimist only on the outside, inside me the lights are always on. Like I know unicorns are crunchy as nuts, and I cry because they are too mythical to eat. I know I can't wade into water, but an animal jumping into a pool in a jungle on a hot day takes my place, that's my splash.

'My retracing of steps is childish, even this need to make up to people is infantile. But I just can't go on, you must trust me on this. I literally can't move or breathe at times. I just want to get out of my bed and talk to this person or that person then and there, set things right. It's like a gun to the head!'

I put on my employee face. 'Finding this woman won't be difficult.'

Nena looked at me, looked away, and when she looked again, she was her composed self. 'That's what I thought.'

My insubordination was an iffy thing, it lacked willpower and a dictionary.

But first, she said, we find my brother. 'I know where the maid lives only in the context of where I used to live. We must go to my parental home and say hello to my only brother.'

Where were her parents?

Her eyes unblinking on the vista. 'Where they always are. In each other's arms.'

~

This story begins where other stories end—in a happy place, with songs and smiles. Two children. Loving family. No raised voices between father and mother. They all, it is said, ate from the sameplate. The siblings were married off to spouses of choice and settled down in rainbows. Life was lovely. If you want to leave the story, the time would be now.

'I have something to say,' the daughter's husband says to her. He has just returned from one of his trips, during which he had a chance to visit her childhood home. 'I found letters your parents wrote to each other in the shoe closet of the room I slept in.'

What can she say? Her parents' love story is

the only one she knows. They were low-key people, the quiet kind, un-shy only in their love for each other. Their bedroom often embarrassed the average hypocritical member of the masses. With its heart-shaped red footstools and whip on the wall, the mirrors on the ceiling and the fat candles dripping wax. She had caught them looking at each other many a times. It was a look she understood even as a child. It spoke of closed bedroom doors and rummaging in kitchen for something to eat, of long hours as an orphan before one by one they grew visible again and slid back into their roles as father, as mother. They were each other's worlds and she was not going to admit to anyone, least of all her cold-eyed analyse-everything-down-to-atoms-and-a-molecule husband, how non-inclusive all that loving had made her feel in the past. She belongs to the breed of matrimonial liars who erase whole histories to self-serve.

'I stole one, just for fun.'

She continues to sew, not looking up at her husband, standing with his legs slightly apart. He takes out something from his pocket and thrusts it at her. A long pink page with cursive flourishes. A love letter dated last month.

She scans it, sucking her thumb where she pricked it, her eyes going over the familiar endearments and undying declarations, flinching at the sensual tone, the frank allusion to their bodies, the mentions of sexual release. Written by one parent of hers to the other.

So they were earthy people with raw honest passion between them. Lust equally felt was a force of nature. Side-effects just happen to include offspring. Peacocks dance to mate, not please passers-by into saying I want a feather. No, no, she was used to this tunnel vision of her parents when it came to each other. Nothing about their hunger for each other surprised her.

Perhaps her husband, in his own inarticulate way, was asking her why her passion for him fell short. Why their bedrooms were on different floors. Men who turned to other women did so with the confidence that their wives waited at home patiently for them. And here she was, unable to provide him with that surety.

It is not me, he was trying to say, it is you. And this is what she wanted to say: It is us.

~

It seems now to me, in my renaissance age, we both came to our virginity from opposite ends; our parents composed us in completely different moods. Hers bursting with lust, mine mute with hate. And though her daughterly heart refused to turn traitor, she knew everyone thought her parents' unabashed desire unhealthy and certainly not acceptable in polite society. She had seen the dark side of that gluttony, how it made minor characters of others.

'Desire was not natural for you or me,' I want to

hold her hand and tell her now. Back then I maintained a cocky silence appropriate to my teenage years.

Terrified by the prospect of finally meeting her brother, Nena gave conflicting directions to the cycle-rickshaw man, who slowly circled around the address given. Where was it, this wretched house of her childhood? I half-expected a fairytale castle to pop up before us, but what we did was go around in empty orbits.

It took her a while to understand what had happened; her brother had sold the house to a builder, who had erected in the place where Nena grew up identical wall to wall white budget villas against the sand like butter spread on bread.

She was baffled. This possibility had never crossed her mind. I think she had fond hopes of making up with her brother—who wouldn't? With the passage of time, one cooks up all kinds of miracles in their mind—of forgiving him grandly, of getting a satisfactory explanation for his cold-blooded homicide of her books. Instead, she was left with a long straw in her mouth and plenty of plain air to suck.

She crooked a finger at me, asking the cycle-rickshaw man who kept rolling his eyes at us useless moneyed lot, to wait for fifteen minutes instead of the earlier shuffling. ('We could take an hour, maybe two, we may spend the night there and return only tomorrow morning, afternoon, oh, I wish I knew.')

Taking my hand—the path was rough, it was getting dark, and she knew the way better than me—she guided me over a low billowing basin, in which lay her river like a teardrop on the cheek of earth.

She sank to her knees. I continued to stand, as copying her posture would mean pretending to be as strung out. She faced the setting sun and, in a voice clear as a bell, said, 'My parents loved each other so much they looked exactly like each other. They were related, of course, distant cousins, as most couples of the time—to keep property within the family. I was born in this house, this house that is no more. Built by my grandfather, it was the tallest and the biggest house, a house befitting me.' She smiled. I couldn't smile back, as anything synthetic would have been the last straw to break her story's back and scatter it to the winds.

'My grandfather said he never willed it to my parents. Every room, every wall, every stick of furniture, I thought it all belonged to me, because I grew up listening to him. The first time I heard of me getting married and going away some day, I ran to him crying. That's true, my grandfather said, you will have one more home, but this will also be your home. Your first home will always be here waiting for you.

'Then my parents did the clichéd thing and made another baby as soon as they could, a baby boy this time. *Sapo de otro pozo.*'

A single child, I have many times decried the

loneliness my selfish parents bestowed on me by not breeding before me—since my father's demise excluded them breeding after me. My childhood had been unbearable, it had been too...adult. Hard labour, missed meals, bleeding arteries, songless words and no courtyard to play in. And here her moaning about *having* a sibling, about too much privilege. I had neither a stance nor speech, so I just continued to stand there, watching the sky make its way down on my head all grim and grey.

'Anyway,' she sniffed, 'this is where I used to come to read—my mother was always scolding me for reading too much, too long, so I had to hide to read. My brother took after my mother, books were the enemy. They thought it too much, what they already knew, and drew the line at anymore knowledge. He must have always wanted to do this, now that I think of it, throw away my books.'

'Yes,' I said, for I had said nothing for a long while and in a person not yet dead that could be considered odd. I sensed her eyes on me, a fine shift in tensions; how much silence is too much listening? 'I lived a different life,' I admitted gruffly.

'What has life to do with living? Life is just presence, existence. Living's the beating heart, kissing mouth, running feet, the unquiet truth-telling tongue. Every awareness of all there is. Not food, it's the appetite. Not music, it's the dancer's feet. Life is you and me where we used to be. Living is us here.'

Even at the time of hearing her say this, even without the mountain of years between then and now that I have to climb higher and higher with slower and slower feet as the days pass, I knew I had to have misheard, that I had begun to contribute my own unused vocabulary to reframe her sentences for myself. Aquiline against the moving shadows that day, skirt windswept, words water vapour. Many a times, I suspect, I've imagined her speech and mine. Like two statues that spoke when no one was watching.

~

The marketplace was a vast cauldron, everything under the sun on sale here. Nena bent to each ware with the air of a connoisseur and haggled excitedly over worthless baubles passing themselves off as gems. Clowns and human curios were announced with deafening drumbeats. Up ahead midgets sat in a circle playing cards, oblivious to gawking children, some who steadily threw stones at them. A woman nursed a baby with four arms and four legs; it must fetch a handsome price on display. Neither Nena nor I stopped at the acrobats' tent, where underfed children with huge eyes sat in sparkly costumes, awaiting their turn on the tightrope, to walk high against the sky with pot upon pot balanced on head. Bejewelled beasts paraded for religious alms, seasonal fruits piled high, salted berries in paper cones, baby fish swimming in transparent pouches, birds hopping about on a leash, frog legs frying, clashing music from buskers... the sounds roaring down at us like lions as we waded down the middle.

We walked on. Nena had a map in her mind of where we'd find that maid, that maid who'd better have begotten a baby or else! Through a forest and past a hutment we were told was haunted, we went. I had half a mind to suggest we explore it, go in and feel the chills if any, but Nena's steadfast pace as well as my inherent inability to feel chills changed that half of my mind. In a clearing we sat cross-legged and finished off the rest of the snacks with us. I know she halved the portions but my memory stops there, what we ate or how much I cannot say. Street food she was especially partial to, scooping up wherever possible a local flavour, demanding I take my share, watching me curiously as I chewed and swallowed, and sighing when I looked neither overwhelmed nor underwhelmed by repasts.

Soon it would be dark, but still she sat dangling her feet above the water till I did the same, like we had all the time in the world, as she chatted away. Our sense of humour, she'd already told me, gave us away; what we laughed at, joked about, revealed who we really were, peeled us down to our core. Perhaps she talked and talked to get me to talk or perhaps she talked and talked so I'd listen. I settled down too in what seemed like the middle of nowhere and gave in to her semi-stories, sub-stories, stories within stories, for everything she said reminded her of something else. Occasionally a silver minnow arced in the distance.

Suddenly she looked around, surprised by the lack of light. 'I can't see you,' she stated.

We stumbled towards a faraway star in the distance. In under an hour, we had reached the borders of the next village. An unsmiling man blocked our path. Who be us, he demanded to know, and she told him a cock and bull story in which we became an old woman and her mentally ill grandson in search of long-lost relatives who'd feed us for the rest of our life.

All the while eyeing us suspiciously, he said it would take three hours on foot and one hour by cart to pass through this village.

We can pay to rest for the night, Nena offered, voice neither hard nor soft. A voice that stood its ground.

In the end we did not have to pay. Escorted silently to what looked like their guesthouse for dignitaries, we were told to make ourselves at home. Uneasy but exhausted we sank into our mats.

The next morning we were back on our path after a strange breakfast of shallots and mustard greens.

8

WITH THE HELP of names Nena could remember in the nick of time, we found the maid's house by and by. The maid was no more, her mother told us.

Symptoms of the illness that bumped off the maid sounded familiar. Emaciation, TB, respiratory hitches, moles and warts, eyeballs swimmy like egg yolks. The mother spoke in hacking fits, and could spit into the distance with ease in the middle of conversations.

AIDS was unmanageable without money or medicine. They had just let the girl die, as if that was the only kindness they could think of.

Hmmm, said Nena, wracking her brains for what to say, what to say. 'When she came back from my house, did she have any complaints?'

'She came back with this illness, big sister.' Though the lady was older than Nena, the latter's bank balance and pedigree made her the 'elder' of the two. 'First she looked happy. But.'

'Anything else? Did she talk about her days there?'

The old woman hesitated; she sensed a largesse coming and wanted no carelessness to alter its path. 'She was very happy there. She said big sister and big brother took such good care of her.'

Nena's eye, the one I could see standing to her right, filled up. One could see the dead girl worked to the bone and hung out to dry, with no maternal figure to ask her how she was, not once. 'Was there a...child?' Her voice wobbled.

This time the old woman was happy to shake her head. 'No baby, big sister. She was not married, then how baby?'

'How baby' was a biology lesson for another day. Nena said okay, fished out a bundle of cash and gave it to the old woman. There was immeasurable grief radiating from her.

The old woman touched Nena's shorn head in blessing, but snatched her hand away as if stung. 'Your head's a cactus! Did you use this new thing called the shampoo that the kids around here have started to buy from the city shops?'

Nena hesitated and then nodded.

'That's just pesticide, big sister. Murders hair! Don't worry, it will all grow back big black thick long in a month, just use this.'

She went into her hut and brought with her a small pouch. Nena took it with suitable reverence. As we walked away from the cluster of thatched huts, I voiced a nagging doubt, 'Are you by any chance hoping to hold a squirming baby in your arms at the end of all this?'

She took a deep breath. 'If there is one, I must make amends. If the baby was born during the time I was married to *Someone*, then I need to atone. If not for me it would have had a father. I can't come between blood and blood.'

It sounded very noble, and nobility suited her more than it did other people, but one can't miss the wonky. Her head seemed transparent to me just then. She was after her husband's child. Pretend to herself she hired a surrogate in the past, when all he really did was run amok behind her back. Maybe he left her, maybe her baby died, maybe she was lonely...

She burst out—'I went *too far, too far*. He lived life king-size, did all his human nature asked of him. I? I hid in that marriage. I hid from all men in that marriage. He was my stab at normalcy, to pass myself off as any other woman. He was...shortchanged. I couldn't bring myself to be this...wife person everyone talks about. The least I can do is find him his baby. If there is one.'

A baby, if you took sanity into account, middle-aged by now. Calling it a baby was her ruse to keep the size of the search small. 'Do you have a child?' This had been on my mind for a long time, and it was a routine question to ask married women.

That's a difficult question to answer, she said. 'Have you felt your child is out there somewhere looking for you? Born to you through a crooked zigzag route because you are lazy, and never stand still. It wants to be your child but you don't let it.'

Not a muscle moved on my face. What she spoke of was way beyond my tender years and perhaps gender. I'd heard my mother rue the physicality of motherhood and here was Nena on the spirituality of mothering, as if children were loose ends you forgot to tie up. I knew I had to move my mouth, make it comment, click tongue in oh-I-got-it. 'You miss the child you are yet to have, will never have.'

Like I miss water, she said. 'Oh, yes, I fantasise about drinking water all the time, isn't that a given? I wake up from deep sleep sure water is on my tongue, in my throat, a fountain in my gut. So many times I've thought to hell with it and sat down with a tumbler filled with water in my hand. I bring it close to my nose, inhale, swirl it around in the steel, and then pour it on my nettles who drink it for me, their porcupine thorns quivering. I'm told,' she said wistfully, 'no one can describe the taste of water. It is the opposite of cyanide, which you taste and die. But water keeps you alive with no record of its flavour.'

Quenches thirst, Nena, that's all, I said, a little embarrassed on her behalf at the aqua opera. 'Babies are a different matter.'

She didn't move, but you got the sense she had flounced off. 'You think this a wild goose chase, don't you?'

Did I? True that she confided only the barest details to me, details that came at me as we went along, but the crux of her journey, the reason she galloped about, did not matter to me at all. I was here because I had nowhere else to be. I flashed a yes/no smile she was free to take how she liked.

'My role models are fictional,' she owned up a little shame-faced, 'Characters in books. The real world I care little about. I live in storybooks.'

~

Once upon a time time there lived a little girl like no other. Every whim indulged, all trees climbed, cycling up dirt tracks one day, climbing down a hill another day, flying kites, hair uncombed, face unwashed, knees skinned, elbows knocking down the priciest vase in her father's collection. She had adventures all day long, and said, when asked, she would grow up to be an adventurer.

By the time she was thirteen she was conceited in the sweetest way; she answered back, she argued, she fought. She knew her languages well, if not her math. She knew how a country was spelt though she hadn't been there yet. She could quote poets dead or alive.

There was no word that scared the girl, no passage she couldn't recite from a book. Her looks were all about her mind, what she said, how she stood her ground and, oh, the way she listened if you knew what you were saying. A psychological acrobat, she could read her way into any mind. Watch out, she'll swing into your subconscious a line of thought you were yet to think.

In such circumstances her goodness was a given. She laboured so long and so hard over what she thought and said and felt and expressed that keeping her body to herself came naturally. This was aided and abetted by the times she lived in. Her religion, the legends retold, the morality tales, the bad things that happened to bad people and the good things that happened to good people rolled into the virtues prized above all when it came to women. A prude par excellence, she surpassed all expectations by keeping herself pure, the purity covering her like enamel did a healthy tooth.

She remembered distant relatives whisper to each other when they thought her asleep; they were talking about how her parents couldn't seem to keep their hands off each other. How disgusting! How embarrassing! 'The things a body makes us do!' they laughed to each other snidely. And she decided then and there to be steered by her mind.

She ran away to a convent nearby. The nuns, however hard she begged, refused to hand over 'just someone's used habit'. They didn't tell her the first thing that came to their mind, which was that she was of another religion, and that her request would mean baptisms and parental consent, which was never going to be given. They did say the second thing that came to their mind, and to them the more important of the two.

'You keep saying,' said the Mother Superior in an almost baritone (for there was no need to lower or caramelise voice when no men were around), 'that you feel nothing for boys. This is not a shelter for girls who feel nothing. It is for those who feel everything there is to feel and who control, conquer and channelise those feelings into their service to God and humanity.'

She was disgusted by this argument. It did not add to her feeling of inherent superiority. She did not want, she was never going to want, men. What was there to want about men?

The nuns were unimpressed, unwelcoming. They all had a man in their life, Jesus.

She ran out feeling as betrayed as she would ever feel her entire life; no abandonment by anyone in the future would override this feeling of being cheated. If what she had thought until now was not true—women as allies—then was man not an adversary either? If you can't trust women, should you start trusting men?

Back home a subtle feminisation was engineered. Her mother, who exerted a hypnotic influence over her father, whispered in her father's ears. It was time to learn flower arrangement, jewellery designing, sit at a piano and paint the sunset. They took away her drums and handed her a violin. She was by now a willing accomplice in this effort at self-civilisation, as she was bored and impulsive enough to be malleable. Perhaps she did want to be accomplished like the heroines of the books she read. It was a challenge; she would be wanted, she decided by and by, though she wouldn't ever want.

Unmarried girls had to always be chaperoned, they were considered terminally ill, and people walked a little away from them as if afraid they'd catch something. A couple of spinsters she met were reluctant virgins, blaming their plainness and lack of dowry for their sorry state. They were not, like her, committed to bodily hygiene. Tch, tch, she went when yet another woman fell into male arms on page number 206.

She blew a raspberry. All right then, she would marry. Find me a man, she told her bleary-eyed parents at breakfast. It was only after a suitable groom was located that her curiosity was piqued. She was told that world-famous lie, she was told about love. That it would steal over her in fluffy clouds, in the pinks and peach of the organzas she so favoured in curtains, it would infuse her spirit like hibiscus tea leaves did hot water. That she would one day on her own want someone. She liked the idea that her body would have a mind of its own and argue with her. If that happened, she would see. She'd be faithful, of course, her fidelity was congenital.

There came a long engagement, then a long separation from her new husband, as he built and built the best nest for her in a city far, far away. His heartfelt disinterest in who she was and where she came from and what was she doing and where was she going. Then the finger that slid slowly down her bare arm one night...

She had tried, she had really tried, to be a good wife. To accept him in her mind and in her body. Every night she heard him come up the stairs, she would try to ignore her pounding heart and come slowly down the stairs with a smile, having rehearsed so many times. There was that evening he came home early and she was downstairs tending to some trivial domestic detail, and he had said something funny, which made her laugh and accidentally brush against him. He had held her hard. She had barely recovered from the feel of his arm around her waist when he bent his face to hers. She saw it approach in slow motion, this face of his. The stubble, the cleft in his chin, the tip of his tongue, coming closer. And she willed herself to stay still. Too late. He had already seen the abject fear in her eyes. With a sigh he sat her down. He explained what they were going to do in some detail, and she heard it like she would any story at bedtime. Like it happened to other people in other places.

But when he bent his face to hers again, she squealed and shook herself free. Though she tried to cover up with light remarks about the latest househelp, he stared at her with no particular expression. Then, as was his habit, he abruptly turned away from her and went to his room.

She sat in the dark, not bothering to light a lamp, and thought about the surrender he spoke of. If she wasn't so terrorised by the very thought of another body upon hers, she would have laughed outright at the comic spread-eagle of it. It was what he said they had to do. No, it was having to do all of that with him. Or. It was her. She who couldn't. For the first time she began to think of can as can't, of her precious virtue as possible vice. Of her very organic inborn repulsion, her unequivocal *no*. That famous control, her disinterest, the halo only she could see around her head now a source of shame. Purity hardened into a hard ball in the pit of her stomach, soured her saliva. Here comes a fault in her own inner mechanism. It was she who didn't know the most intricate step in a universal dance.

She couldn't. She wouldn't. I won't, she said, I can't.

9

'IF A BODY won't comply, we give it to god or pimps. It has to go to someone, anyone. That's the law.' She sighed, and patted the wiry hair on her head. 'Whoever heard of keeping it vacant just for the fun of it?'

I knew it was optional that I respond. My objection to life itself was its demand that we react to it 24/7. It places a hand on our forehead—'How are we today?' The thermometer must come away 104 degrees. Excitable the same as *alive*.

Nena's tales of her husband's adultery affected women two ways—one type of woman sees herself as the wife and takes sides, one type of woman identifies with the other woman and stays to hear how it ends. My own mother was neither; all she wanted to do was borrow a bit of Nena's sass, her boldness, bask in her rebellion. Like a blind person who could slowly start to see, she put away her cane—deities and altars and beads and bells—and tottered out into the sunlight. Her spine slowly uncurled, speech stopped curdling on her tongue. She started liking the sound of her own voice; 'I,' she started to say more and more often, 'I'. Planting herself in her stories where she could see herself. If she did not jump off a cliff when I decided to drop out for a year, it was because Nena herself looked placid at all times, and my mother wanted to try some of that placidity. A recess in one's own life, a time to do nothing but wait and watch, like a bridge between two parts of your life, one lived, one unlived.

Owning up to your inertia, not enough shrines built to it. 'Can't' was the word Nena used. The word stuck in the throat like a fishbone, the 'no' that says itself. A visceral inability to nod even though it will destroy lives and whisk the earth from under your feet. You shake your head with a raw grief, knowing they see you now as an ingrate, as stubborn, while you are only being you.

~

Next on the list was the cook who was also the lover. Remember? she asked me, I told you about her.

'The first story you told me,' I reminded her in turn.

She had only some phonetic sounds to divulge the name of the village, the most molecular of clues. 'He said', 'But then', 'What about', 'Look for'...We twittered about as usual, like mahouts given mice instead of elephants to mount.

It had a post office, she said, because *Someone* always waited for letters from his parents. His aunt was a strict woman who allowed him to read them only once a month, having told the postman to bring all of them together in a bunch on the first of every month. What *Someone* did was steal out during after-school hours, ambling towards the only post office, and read the letters in secret. The postman, a young father himself whose children were being brought up by his wife and her family somewhere far away because he was transferred here, obliged him happily both at the post office as well as home, where he would bring the letters with a suitably solemn air to the fire-eyed aunt. Who was of the opinion that softness to children, including allowing them to read sentimental letters from foolish parents, spoilt them.

From the postman the boy learnt that Government was the wicked witch in every fairytale. It controlled and interfered with your life and happiness. The Government had cast away the postman here, miles and miles from his hometown. The Government kept the boy's own parents somewhere else too. That's what the Government did, keep families apart. It was anti-love. That his aunt praised the Government all the time only added to their distrust, and brought man and boy closer together.

Dhoop of course wasn't the cook's name, so evocatively curling the boy's tongue unto old age in one of Nena's tales.

She came to cook in their house from...we drew a blank. The house itself was high on a hill in...another blank. The aunt was...Her name was...She lived in... blank blank blank.

I voiced what we were both thinking. 'This is a little impossible.'

Nena was distraught. What do we do, what do we do. What? Do? We? Do?

'Are you crying?' I peered at her.

She stamped a foot. 'You know I can't! Tears make the lashes fall off my eye.'

~

The unborn see us just as we see the born. Floating frozen in the unknown. Shooting stars blinding bright, leaving behind such grief and helplessness, questions and a dense loss, a loss that locks all doors behind it. Will we see them again, these embryos with their noses pressed against the windowpane?

In a reverie he came to me, this child who would be mine. And I followed on silent footsteps, lest it sensed me and dissolved. The farther it walked, the nearer I got. As long as I could see it, I knew it was mine, that it had come for me. It smells the ghost milk in my breast.

But who would make it? Who would set aside the time and the love, the beauty and the patience, to start him for me, my son?

He is here. I recognise him in my sleep, a face more familiar than mine. He does not know but I do. I will find him where he is.

~

I kept my expression neutral. 'Do you hate your husband that much?'

She was taken aback. 'Hate him? Not at all. In fact, I understood him from the start. It is me I don't understand. I am the aberration, he is the normal one. Tell me, what is unnatural about using your body for pleasure? I envy him, truth be told. You have to forgive marriages and their childish rules...Monogamy is a lovely dream, but lust has only one partner it is faithful to forever—the body.'

'And this cook will give you...what? You will pay her some money, close the loop and feel good about yourself?'

'She will give me any child she bore my husband, that is what she will do.'

But she must be a grandmother by now, the son a father himself. They may have done so well for themselves that they won't need any handouts. Or they may be proud people, who do not like the idea of strangers married to any illicit lovers they may have temporarily taken in a weak moment reaching them with offers to pay off debts. She would, with her assertions, and that too only going by an old husband's old recollections, cause grievous damage to their mask of morality.

Nena seemed nonplussed by the idea that years and years had passed. Eyebrows at two different levels, she looked at me like I was refusing to wind the clock.

'Who wants,' I tried to ask her without too many words, with very little sound, and only because it was high time she was made to see sense, 'strangers you don't know to suddenly appear in your life and point fingers at an action of yours you think no one knows about? Even if every suspicion of yours is as real as you'd like it to be, it would still be a calamity for this family. Paternities will have to be shuffled, blood will have to be partitioned. You know this deep down, which is why your memory has blocked all allusions that can help you to find this woman and any child she may have had. Yes, she came to your husband naked and crying over an empty lap, but the infertility could have been hers, in which case even your ever-virile husband could not have impregnated her.'

'I can be discreet,' she said but the fight had gone out of her.

Startled by my own verbosity, I missed out her reticence, her deflated hmmm and mmmm. It was the longest I ever spoke to her, it was the longest I ever spoke to anyone. The words squatters on my tongue I just had to evict. Which word when—I had to arrange in a way they stood according to height.

She straightened agitatedly and smoothed the sides of her robe-like dress that went all the way down to her feet and flapped around her ankles. By now enough changes of clothes had happened and we were well-versed with each other's couture. Who *are* you, she asked, not for the first time and not a question I have an answer to even today.

My stillness, my disability when it came to setting myself into motion, seemed to rile her. I did a bad thing, she said.

~

It wasn't any particular day or time. Just another mid-week bustling menace of endless hours when she lectured the servants, planned the menu, tended to the garden and went about her sundry self-assigned chores. The laundry was what she was thinking idly of tackling next when she heard her husband come in. She knew his mood at once, despondent.

'A girl I know got herself pregnant,' he said. There were sweat beads on his nose.

She didn't ask too closely who 'a girl' was. Or whose 'a girl' she was. 'A girl' was no one to do with her or with him.

He said, 'She comes from a conservative family and a boy plucked her like a ripe grape. You know boys. He won't marry her and her parents will kill her if they know. You have to do something.' There can't be a scandal, he said. In some dim recess of her mind, it did occur to her that her husband may be more involved than he let on, but she was also aware that her future was tied up with his. He was to contest elections, he was en route to greatdom, and who knows whose baby it was? Who can say with this type of girl?

Abortions were illegal and only the seediest of quacks would do this for you, and that too at a price they quoted at will, so she had to take the young, frightened thing to a dilapidated building in a lower-status area and get this done hush-hush.

When she met the girl, in a dim corner of a deserted building, she was taken aback by the vivid swell of her stomach. She had not expected it, despite the secretive reason for their meeting, this big rise of her belly. She was aware she should say something, alleviate the girl's abject terror at what was going to happen, but she stayed silent, distant. She would do this, but only for her husband. The girl was immaterial. Indeed, she was wholly replaceable. She was without past, future, face or name. Why commit to memory what she looked like when they would never meet again? Girls such as these who did not take care of themselves did not deserve her politeness or manners.

She sat out there, having delivered the girl unto an airless ultra-bright chamber, after placing the thick bundles of cash on the 'doctor's' desk even as he protested that the risk was too high, the foetus too far gone etc. She tried to feel all accomplished, like she always did whenever she rose to the occasion, any occasion. To cope with what life threw at you, that was a talent, an art, and she congratulated herself each time she met squarely what she could have ducked.

Mother of god, what was that? A low keening seeped through the walls to where she sat, smothering her decibel by decibel in excruciating slowness. An animal cry. Wrenched from the dying baby or from its living mother, she didn't know, she didn't care. Like a cry for help from hell.

It cut her down like grass.

An assistant in home clothes came out afterwards and told her it was over. Coated in sweat she jumped up then to go in and take the girl home, wanting to be out of here as soon as she could, but was told the girl could not be moved right away, maybe tomorrow?

She left without hesitation. She had done her job. There was no need to go in and see the girl, who must be sedated or sleeping.

The girl bled to death the same evening. Her husband was shivering a little when he told her this. He poured himself a large drink, and she was anxious for him, his blood pressure, his nerves. Darling, she said, it happens.

The death was tragic of course, but girls who

danced too close to the flame would be moth sooner or later.

~

I felt a compulsion to cough up comfort words. But Nena saved me the spurious pity by saying, 'That wasn't the bad thing I did.'

10

AS WE PUT up our feet, with nowhere to dash off to for the moment, Nena began to plan picnics. She met people familiarly, lovingly, with such avid interest in their life, that you could actually see them preen like peacocks. They hardly saw me by her side, someone who organised the tea, asked for the bill, left a tip...I was sure that for all those who happened to see us then we were a study in contrasts, at least I felt this acutely. I imagined them for days afterward asking each other, 'Who was that again?'

She'd wake up all arch looks and manic energy, me with barely a pulse—the she-me seesaw, a travelling circus of two. And between us that silence rich with nothing, two mimes resting. I was her alibi, the one who knew she was here on this day, there on that day. Her sayings, in every which language, caught me on the backfoot for want of a context. To insurance seller promising a hundred percent cover in case of death—'Hundred percent *only*?' Bursting into tears mid-read—'Just a book, I know, I know...' Her lamp, she told me, was magical, for it rendered her wish-less. 'When I know I can ask for anything, anything at all, I feel I have everything.'

Passionate confessions, longwinded accounts of betrayal and backstabbing came thick and fast at her, mainly as she had appointed herself as personal listener to the world. Tell me, she said to anyone who passed by her, and they told her. Then it was payback time—they had to listen.

Nena traded in tales, told and retold them. Stories rained day and night, soaking us to the skin. Her mouth never tired. I heard the same story once, twice, ten times, but the sorcery never stopped. Voice lowered to pure bass, beating like drums in bloodstreams, entering intravenously, leading astray little girls and grown women alike. I watch the rapt faces around the fire; flames light up a teary eye, a wobbly lip. I could feel their body heat, their fever, as their feet gripped the magic carpet.

~

Best to leave a place when its sights were still wondrous, with nothing, not even the sunrise, commonplace. Was that why Nena left my hometown, because the scenery staled? I was dead sure by now of her decision to never return there, to wisp into smoke. It was there in the cosy way she snuggled into strange furniture in wayside inns and budget motels, and once in a while, as a treat for me, some luxury home-stay. We were still meeting people and inching along a pathless route. Those who knew her and those who didn't, she met them all. I watched her without looking at her. Those were the days I lifted a shoulder, rubbed jaw, clicked teeth or tilted head in lieu of speech. Except for the rare impassioned words that burst out of me when she provoked me enough, I was a mumbler, talking not even to myself. Of course, the usual motherly snapping never took place between us; she never said eat more, drink not, bathe quick, sleep less. Most of the time the age difference never interfered, even though she'd say—In my time. In those days. Back then. We used to…She made it the one superpower she had, the many years she had lived before me. Pulling rank. Maybe I was too young to be ageist (after all, I was brought up by a single mom, and for all the hatred I spewed against her, I was used only to her).

When I look back at our time together, my memory uses crayons. I see her, I see me, and everything around us a child's drawing. As we sat by a fireplace with cartoon flames, she pulled out some papers from her bag. The papers were currency notes. For you, she said.

Knowing how much bringing me along with her had cost her in terms of tickets and food and rent, I blinked. For me?

And then I felt a pang; is this the end?

We are going next to...she named where my college was located.

Was this the deal between my mother and you? I asked coldly. Was that why she jumped with joy when I left with you?

Not at all, she owned up, my plan entirely.

Classes were due to start in a month. And I was not yet sure—though I knew I had no choice really—whether I wanted to return. Return to what? Return as who?

In barter she said, 'Let me tell you the bad thing I did.'

~

She was by now less a stunner, more a slob. New rare designs from exclusive boutiques did not set her pulses racing like they used to. Handbags had become less about aesthetics, more sacks to throw things into. Conversation itself, if she wasn't the one speaking, put her to sleep. She became more and more house-bound. She liked to potter about her lawns, talk to plants an irridescent jade, chat with servants, now more like old friends, and read, of course. That never stopped, despite glaucoma and an ophthalmologist warning her of complete blindness soon; she just held the book closer to her face. Books were bought from all corners of the world, they came tumbling into the house with their pages flying. She raided libraries like looting plunderers of yore, and had an underground network of second-hand buyers and first edition sellers who reported directly to her.

That was the closest she came to the sensual, when a book she hadn't read yet landed in her bare hands. She'd caress it all over, eyes softly shut, hold it against her face and inhale deeply. Mine, she'd say with a possessive thrill, all mine. Written for me to read. Touch at its most skinless.

More and more she felt this urgency to story-tell.

A bird pecked my throat to
transfer secret seed to
germinate in whispers to
flower in bushy reds to
grow wild forests on
unopened earths.
I keep it in my cheek, don't swallow.

She left it pending, her habit of spinning yarns, a secret between her and her, like she was going to go behind her own back one day. But instinctively she knew she would open her mouth and that would be that. Stories would tumble out all drunk from being untold until then.

Her husband went about his life much as an unimpeded bachelor would. He had told her on the day she arrived here, as a young bride, 'Only one person can rule a household. I have seen many families ruined because both the man and the woman compete to be the head. We shall not go that way.'

We shall not, she soothingly murmured, knowing that it did not matter who ruled as long as she could roam free. He could call himself king, she was no kingdom.

While he set himself up as her lord and master, she let him believe in her veneration. She thought him puny for setting up one-sided rules that benefit the rule-maker. It was easy to look down on him in the privacy of her head, this man who misunderstood her from scratch.

The formative years of the marriage she dedicated to setting him right in her own way. His moods—tendency to criticise, to lose temper, to 'correct' her for her own good, to educate her even—were quickly dealt a death blow. No ranting, no furniture destroyed, but there was about her a sturdy indifference. She refused to be shaken by anything he said or did. Instead, she stood shoulder to shoulder, an ally, someone he knew it was in his interests to trust.

Women filing paternity suits were routinely sent packing by her, with some money, the promise of a job. Lies, he said, all lies. And she played along docilely. Maybe they were never his, the stillborns or those who escaped the midwife's hand. He did insist on a diet heavy in okra, to kill his seed with the gossypol in it...It mattered not if he was dallying; besides, their coffers were overflowing. She dwelt not on the rising number of unwed mothers making their way to her, she doled out instead advice their mothers should have given them—stay away from dodgy men. Stay. Away.

Her husband was not to be disturbed—not only because he did not want to be disturbed but because she wanted, above all, to forget he existed in the first place. They led parallel lives in the greatest of harmonies. Sticky taffy with guests around; he touched her elbow over her sleeve and she let him. He, in turn, learnt to pretend a great respect for her he did not feel. He praised her family name, good taste, charity work, inauguration of schools. 'Dearest,' he'd say, voice the pulp of tender coconuts, 'tell them about the time you visited the orphanage and decided to bring all the orphans back home with you.' And thus they would have gone on, prompting each other in perfect unison and marital PR till death claimed one of them—if not...

...if not for that night they fought like cats and dogs. A great blackness descended upon them from nowhere and one thing led to another till she mocked his gullibility in thinking all his conquests anything but trapped women. 'You think they love you? Can you be loved, ask yourself that. They are actresses acting on the great stage of your bed.'

He listed every fruit every woman had made of herself just for him, like succulent peaches clad in lingerie that bared nipple, crotch; how delectably they arranged themselves on his bed, on his office desk, on his lap. How they reached out for him not just behind closed doors but in public places, panting so hard for him they did not care who saw, who heard. Acts they denied doing with anyone but him, only for him. He was their demon lover, their carnal nemesis, the man who left them starchless and limp after he had his way with them. They did not walk for weeks.

Please, she scoffed, don't brag about lies paid women tell you. What is so great about a woman dancing naked because she's strapped for cash? Come and tell me when a woman dances naked because she is too excited to stand still or keep her clothes on around you.

'I have booked honeymoon suites in every motel along the highway.'

Oh, the pubic hair shed on rented beds!

'My staying power is legend, I am harder than... than stone.'

Ha, confusing genitals with heart.

You like men dead waist down.

I like men alive neck up.

'Frigid cow!' he snarled. 'Your cunt sleeps like a baby.'

You think your penis is you, you use it like a battering ram, to bully, because without that force, without that constant motion of your hips, you are nothing, nobody. Just a man with women who say yes to any man. A man set up in the world by his wife so he can flaunt her wealth and call himself a stud.

By now they were standing very close, almost touching as they talked. He shoved her, she fell against a desk, her temple split open and she felt the sticky wetness of blood. It made her a little woozy and lose her place in the argument. 'What?' she said, bewildered. 'What?'

'Show me,' he said yanking her knees apart with careless force, 'show me this treasure you have been hiding from the whole world, for which no man is ever good enough.'

She was half-sitting half-lying on the floor, all the more easy for him to unbutton his fly, sweep her long satin skirt out of the way and jam himself against her.

She almost lost consciousness. She had never actually felt anyone ever, no skin against her skin, no body against her body, nothing and no one ever upon her privatest, where she was at her most clandestine, most church-mouse poor. She had never been up against what was so obvious, so vulgar, so twitchy. For a moment she thought his heart had fallen out of his shirt to beat in her lap.

She gave way like old parchment. 'This temple built between your legs!' he mocked. Grabbing both her legs with hard hands he forced them up his shoulders, biting a foot when she tried to kick the side of his head. 'I should have done this long ago! I am getting inside of you, stop me if you can, you...you nothing but a woman!' he grunted, tightening his hold around her neck, pressing down on her mouth with a calloused hand. The pastel curtains in the room seemed to catch fire before her eyes. Air corked her nostrils. He was all show, don't tell—*I* who can penetrate *you*.

She used all of her might to put a hand on the desk to somehow drag herself up, to stand and end this evil between them, because this was not them, they were almost friends, were they not? But what her hand encountered was the paper knife, burnished gold and sharp as a cleaver, she kept there to slit open the stuck pages of newly printed books. (She so hated to tear them unevenly and spoil the looks of books.) Grabbed and brought down with all her might; he didn't see the glint...She slashed blindly again and again at that part of him that was trying to touch her at her most untouchable.

He screamed one long scream. For quite some time she thought it came from her throat. That unbroken howl of single sound. Then she threw the knife where he could see and told him with raised empty hands, look, I stopped, I stopped, can't you see?

And still he screamed.

~

Nena wiped her crew-cut hair in short sharp strokes as if shaking out rain. 'It is true I invested heavily in prudery like all women of good breeding do. They called me innocent.' She turned to me earnestly. 'Innocence is a sin, ignorance acting coy.'

I coughed. She returned in a flash to where we had left him.

'I stood there, every screw in my head loose, blood in high tide, and wished with all my might that I could undo what I had done.'

Those days, she said, no such surgery was available. From what she has read since that may require top-class surgeons in state-of-the-art hospitals, the severed part kept on ice, first-aid and someone to suture nerve endings.

His cries for help bounced off the crystal chandeliers, but no one came. No servant dared interfere between man and wife. The nearest neighbour, owing to their affluence, was miles away. He lay there bleeding freely into the exquisitely embroidered carpet and she began to think little housewife thoughts by habit. Ammonia or peroxide, what is best for stains? She waited for the red to stop, but it seemed to her it never would.

All she could do was lock him in that room with his scream.

~

I did not know, said Nena, what to do with what I had done. I wiped and wiped with everything I could lay my hands on, my best evening clothes, my most expensive cocktail dress. But the bleeding wouldn't stop, the screaming wouldn't stop.

I called the family doctor, who was good enough to come in the middle of the night, no questions asked.

Where is he, he asked tersely, and I pointed to that locked room. I sat downstairs, not daring to go up and see him. Was he dead? I hoped he was dead. Without his penis he would not want to live. It was his heart, that organ.

He will live, began the doctor, but he will suffer urethra complications all his life, piss pus, that kind of thing.

I thought about it. He had complicated my life, it was okay that his got a little complicated too. I stayed long enough to mastermind his recovery. I fed him his meals, changed the dressing in his groin, kept out of the way. But before he could limp out of his room somewhat normal, I picked up every gem of jewellery, every note of currency I could, and vamoosed.

I march, my footsteps follow.

'I had thought it impossible,' she said, 'to exist outside of that dream. That house, that garden, the pebbled path, the stained-glass windows, the art-house lamps, fountains and goldfish and love-birds and a tiger cub still on bottle, the slaves I paid a handsome price for and the organic harvest from my own farm—but once I left, I realised I had only been keeping myself out of sight. Walking out of that gate I felt I was stepping into real life, my real home. It was blind trust, an animal knowing, that I would soon find a roof, a floor. I could not see my feet as I walked but that is the thing about feet, they know where to go.'

Did she ever, even for a minute, regret giving up creature comforts, the art, the culture, the high society, playing house?

She said she'd lived in edifices and abodes, turrets and minarets, and called them home for she knew no better. Because one expects shelters to be outside of oneself, spelt out in bricks and hand-picked tiles. Packing and unpacking, settling and moving. You can go from room to room to room and not be home.

That was my marriage, she said. I jumped out but really I just vacated an imaginary place.

And then? And then?

'I found the least humid place on the map and landed up next door to you.'

11

I DECIDE TO run away that night. I could just melt into the world with no one the wiser. I would finally have a say in my own life. From the moment of my birth I owed my existence to another, who birthed me, who fed me, who paid my fees...Why can I not be who I am? Whoever I am to be?

But even as I sat up, I knew I could not go through with it, use the night as a cover for my cowardice. If I was to go, I should tell her to her face—she would never ask me for anything, least of all, a reason. A blackmailer of another ilk.

Agreed, that story was more gripping than any I expected, and I am sure ninety-nine percent factual—but did I sell myself short for a stanza of make-believe? I had no desire to be tugged by hand like a wayward child back to where I ran away from. Why would I? When I left that place, I had vowed I would never return.

~

We landed in my part of the world by and by. There had been no hurry on her part or mine to make our way here, but ever since the destination was decided, I had been trying to mentally prepare for reaching here.

The station looked different, the movie posters had too many female bosoms, passers-by looked one-dimensional. We found a youth hostel this time with bunk beds. She worried it was too short for me, I lied it wasn't though my feet dangled when I lay down. It was the first time we shared a room.

I noticed her feebleness, deflated eyes, slurred speech, flushed cheeks and the spray of rosacea on her cheeks. She also looked more and more lost in her own thoughts; her stories sometimes made no sense. There was a stilted note to our conversation, though on the surface we said all the right things.

I let her go wherever it was by herself for once. I did make a cursory enquiry and she waved a dismissive hand. She was hiding something from me, that was clear. That wad of notes, that glazed eye, the insistence that I get off here, at this stop, the last stop...

I had thought she was ridding herself of me, maybe she was ridding me of her. When she came back she looked tired, like she could not take another step. I told her she should make her way home and that I could take her there.

I don't go anywhere, she said, the journey will take me.

Then why globetrot? Why not stay put if you thought your time had come?

'I only thought, please, I don't want to be in one place like some boring old pensioner. I want to go on the go. Own my death. I even checked out the bridge, you know, and stood there dreaming of jumping. Water will kill me faster than it kills others. But then I thought what if I fell on a ledge head-first, broke all bones and frightened everyone at the funeral? I always think of others first.'

That made me laugh, even as a typeface clacked through my head. (More and more, words sped and whistled through me like a night train, not stopping, not slowing.)

Part soul, part spine, part feather, part beak,
part full, part part. As I jump off parapets
I'm wing and fin, part sky, part sea.

She made as if to place a palm between my shoulder blades, but at the last moment held back so I did not have to move away. 'Just when I started to despair where to go your mother came home and moaned about your untimely return, and I said send him to me. I could see our shadows fall on walls all over the world.'

She was right, of course. I did want to wake up in places I was yet to go.

Her lips darted in quick smile. 'I had a couple of goals, you know them, finding any illicit produce of my husband and to consume water. I knew I'd die of either and I did both.'

But no child had come forward claiming her for a mother or her husband for a father, and water dared not come within drinking distance of her.

She made semi-circles with her head, arching to the left and right. 'I am not a biological mother and I must make peace with that. But I did get to taste water.'

'So...so how does it taste?' Let's call her bluff.

She closed her eyes. 'Like biting snow off the highest mountain peak. Neither cooked nor raw, kind of chewy...if you can get your teeth to stop it long enough.'

I desperately wanted to stop her nonsense thinking; it seemed to me she was psyching herself to die. She would very much like the posthumous reputation of being a soothsayer, that she had predicted her own death right down to the minute. And I was to be her witness till the end, her human loudspeaker, the one who was going to tell everyone back home how she timed her own departure, imagine that. Sometimes she was so transparent she might as well be water. I sighed exaggeratedly. 'So you drank water and so you drank it lots. That happens with water, one never knows when to stop. But how is it your assassin?'

She mimicked my sigh. 'It is everywhere inside of me now. I smell of gunpowder.'

~

Sleep choked me. Nightmares jumbled. Father stamped on my head. Mother hit her own head. I was chased down blind alleys by the headless and the limbless. During the day I was as normal as I always was, largely silent. But when I went to sleep, I kept waking up. Soon my eyes felt distended, like they were walking off my face.

She, on the other hand, looked merrier than ever. As if finally offloading me in planned destination was one more thing off her list of things to do. I am guilty of overlooking her general decline in health, the persistent cough of respiratory origin, the lack of appetite and of lucidity, the bits of bile left behind in the mangy basin. I was fed up with her by now, truth to tell, with her lofty attitude to exhaustion, an indifference that included me in its vacuity. She could barely focus. Started and ended monologues that I affected not to hear, not to follow. I also knew that I was vanishing from her sight, me as I was, however little that be. I now stood in for the larger world, her imaginary audiences, karma, comeuppance. She muttered and whispered at odd times, when she wasn't even sure of my presence, prefixing my name—my wrong name, what she felt like calling me at that moment—to sentences not applicable to me.

The bad thing I did, whom do I tell now?

~

The girl licked her lip looking straight at me. My friends slapped my back. She will let you have her, they said. They said it casually, like it was a given. That I could reach out and there she would be. I catch the glimmer of her from the corner of my eye. She seemed to be covered in sap.

I buried my head in textbooks. Unlike the others who I imagined were heirs to large fortunes, my own circumstances were different, dire. I couldn't afford to fritter away my time. I had to study, study, study. My mother's tears, her past humiliations, her hopes of future prosperity hunched my shoulders. There was no way I could let myself get distracted.

The girl made herself more obvious. There was a look in her eye that assessed me a simpleton, someone unable to pick up signals. We barely spoke, passed each other at assembly. The college had hostels only for boys; girls were day scholars. She appeared mornings, vanished evenings.

But I could not stop to see what was in her gaze.

My classmates here were posh, unlike my more modest companions back home. Here they mistook me for being as rich as them, as able to afford little things like the drugs and drinks sold in secret. I lived a tightrope life, trying to look normal at all times, hoping I would not slip up and let my destitution show.

The girl got bolder, frightening me more. Was I supposed to reciprocate, embrace her in sheer gratitude?

I wished I was the passionate suitor of her dreams, instead I was shaking in my shoes. I wanted her to leave me alone, not even think all those things she said she wanted to do to me, let alone say them so publicly in black and white to me.

Those letters. Each more impassioned than the last. What was she saying? Meant to set me on fire, she spoke of fait accompli, of legendary lovers, of those who eloped and set up shaky domiciles on the very edge of earth. She wanted me all to herself, she wanted me away from everyone and everything I knew; she wanted me, she swore, only me. She said she knew me on sight, recognised me from previous lifetimes. The surety in her words made me giddy. All I felt was the slow start of sadness, for being noticed, targeted and not being able to care one way or the other.

At my wit's end and in sheer carelessness, I let my roommate read one of her missives, then it became a hostel joke, a class joke, a college joke, till everyone was reading her letters as fast as she wrote them.

Her imageries, physical violations; her language borrowed from erotic texts, every line a fantasy, a lie she lived. I held the paper in my hand, scalded by the red-hotness of her passion, and read helplessly.

Quiet as breath exits a body, you enter my room. I don't turn but see. Your palm out to catch me like a raindrop, the length of your eyelash. Your mouth in my hair, my hair in your mouth, I lick my hair to taste what you taste. Your tongue tastes of tempests. I look at you, you are looking right back, and the silence, O the silence, of not a word from you, not a word from me. If death took me now I would know not.

Why did she love me thus? Why did she single me out for her 'love'? I who felt nothing in return.

The boys, unknown to me, started to reply to her as me. When in one of her letters she invited me to a godforsaken barn in the college compound for a rendezvous, they wrote back their immediate assent.

She set a date. My friends, the spoilt brats, the large oil-spill of tycoon sperm, replied to her in my name, saying, yes, I will be there.

I was fast asleep in my bed that night but I should have had an inkling.

~

She walked into the barn heart thudding. She had never been in love before. And there was something so humble about him. Unlike the other boys who managed to look only entitled. This one held in an innate aloneness. She was going to offer everything to him, all she had, anything to rid him of that pain he wore as second skin. Maybe then his defences would crumble and he would gather her to him, at last his mask broken and his speech dedicated solely to her.

~

She was found barely conscious the next morning by the guard's son who went to unlock the barn to pick up the washing. Her clothes were torn, her eyelids puffy and froth ringed her mouth. Left for dead, but breath still tore at her chest. The guard's son made the mandatory hullabaloo that saw her being shifted to a medical facility and a slow, painful reconstruction.

The boys were found out—each one ratted on the other, these sons of their rich fathers—and they were all suspended. If she had died, the principal thundered, they would have been jailed.

Confessions tumbled out. The intercepted letters being read by others, the invite, the plan...

I was blameless, according to her police statement. That was still her 'love' speaking, this exoneration of me when she could not be sure I had nothing to do with her demolition. And me supposed to go on as if nothing happened.

She was sent off somewhere else, to some other college they said, but maybe she never went anywhere again. Food and sleep and studies and the conversations around me ceased. I could see mouths move, hands reach out, but I had backed off from speech and touch, retreated where none could follow. I, who never really knew who I was, moved further away from that knowing.

~

'There is a friend I must meet,' I told Nena.

We made enquiries just like old times, we drew road maps just like before, but we both looked done now. She could not stand for long, I could not sit for long.

I had no idea when we set off, how this would pan out. It was her house we were going to, the girl who said she loved me and paid the price for that loving. There was no guarantee she would be there, of course, but these were holiday months, so a good chance she could be there. A part of me wanted her to be there, so some form of apology could expectorate out of me; another part of me wanted to never meet her, to go through life like she wasn't there in the world at all. Who was she, after all? I had never looked her in the face, spoken to her. I had only seen her in passing; someone who thought herself madly in love with me. Me.

Streetlights flickered. Smog was rolling in.

~

I left Nena waiting in the car, which was just as well, as she was not up to any walking. From the gate to the door was a good five-minute brisk trot. At last I was against my will at her door, pressing her doorbell.

A butler opened the door.

Can I see...I said her name.

She is indisposed, not up to seeing visitors. There was this tragedy, you may have heard.

Tell her it is me...I gave my name.

The butler returned and led me into a parlour, painted gold.

The girl who used to ogle me so brazenly at one time, who thought me the reason she was born, was huddled in a corner chaise longue looking blindly at the floor.

Quiet as breath exits a body, you enter my room.

'The killers you hired are no good. I am still alive,' I say.

I don't turn but see. Your palm out to catch me like a raindrop, the length of your eyelash.

Slight move of head, her hair did the shimmy shake. Like satin giving way to silk.

Your mouth in my hair, my hair in your mouth, I lick my hair to taste what you taste.

'I should have come long back, but I really couldn't...'

She shushed me with her mouth on mine.

Your tongue tastes of tempests.

I heard her speak for the first time, her voice exactly as I imagined it to be.

I look at you, you are looking right back, and the silence, O the silence, of not a word from you, not a word from me. If death took me now I would know not.

If death took me now, I would know not.

~

When I came back to the car, Nena was dozing. I told her what an opulent house it was. Liar, she shot back, you never went in. I was watching you the whole time.

A butler opened the door, I insisted.

No one opened the door. The house has been locked up for ages.

Oh, shut up, Nena.

You were just standing there talking to yourself.

~

On the way back, Nena's head kept lolling back on the seat of its own volition. She was a touch incoherent. 'Imagine when people meet other people and their blood turns to hooch. Laughing when someone loves them, crying when someone leaves them. Bodies crying for bodies.'

Only some of what she said was clear, only some of what was clear I retained.

Let me tell you, she said suddenly sharp, what happens to your girl.

My girl?

This girl. Any girl. A girl.

~

Under my clothes I write my history; blade pen, skin diary. Spun in six yards of skin my own, earth-dusted paisley-printed, I admire my craft in mirrors late at night. Skin a bark I carve your initials on. Bridge I click love locks to, bed I leave unmade. At nights the razor whispers—'Say something, say anything.' Between my collarbones a pendant bleeds. Skin is the largest organ, I give it a tongue. Sonneteer, balladeer, roof over my head, ground beneath my feet, under it I live storm or sun, naked inside, naked outside. A quilt I unpick, the lining slowly gives, follicle by follicle. Welts mean well, the deepest wound just some quiet insipid skin before.

Must call mom, drink less, show strange men the door who follow me home gushing about my body parts. Must feed cat-fish-pup, shower, keep knife off wrist, feet off ledge, eyes off the shawl that can hammock my neck to the fan. Must cry prettily when men ask are you lonely, and say, I'm lonely for you, only for you. Must relearn to growl, my wolves have turned herbivorous. I meet me every day on my doorstep and ask myself at six p.m. if I'd rather stay in or go out and gather some more human dust on my arms.

~

Neither head nor tail, increasingly her stories dissolved into beautiful lines. When the stories in storytellers dry up, only words remain. Nena would not be drawn and I had had enough of enigmatic women. This is what I was going to do with my life, I told her, I was going to never conjecture or ponder. Fiction sucks. It threw up disturbing probabilities without taking responsibility. Fiction masquerading as fact. Facts trying on new clothes. Equally untrue, life and lore.

Nena agreed. Yes, stories were only stories in the end, but they gave us what we never knew we needed. That rainbow in the sky is the sun telling lies. She crossed her arms limply, looking all wiped out. 'Okay, you say. What happens to her?'

'I see her,' I said with pomp and show, 'on a swing in a garden designed by her husband whose job it is to sing lullabies to babies everywhere. The king of that country has put them up in his palace. Every time he has a baby, the lullaby singer sings the little prince or the little princess to sleep. At night he goes back to his pregnant wife and sings to the soft swell of her belly. This goes on for nine months after nine months till all of time ends.'

Your first story, she gasped, but I divined even then that my story was no story. It was my attempt at righting wrongs. No conflict, no resolution, contrived beginning, rushed ending. There was a king in it, a songster and newborn princesses but nothing happened to them. They maintained status quo, a boring thing at best.

I am no storyteller. I don't have the honesties stories demand. Her stories, on the other hand, were a jam jar filled with fireflies, jungles of blue jackals. She seemed to pluck from the air between us something ripe, something ready. The lives she spoke of, the lives I lived, I who had no life. She said as much sometime during our time together—'The listener reaches down the teller's throat for the story.'

No one can deny I was a listener, her listener.

~

Nena, meanwhile, continued to go her way.

She spat up whatever she ate. She could not keep down anything for long. Acid reflux singed her gums. The more she flopped down, arms flailing, the more tight-lipped I got. I was of the firm belief that she must make an effort, must make an effort. Eyelashes tangled, any attempt at speech just a parting of lips. I watched her limp into the bunk bed, and as she pulled a sheet over herself, I found her looking at me. Like she used to. Steady, unblinking, know it all. I stumbled back, impaled. I had forgotten how she could use those eyes, like props in a play.

I kept the lamp where she could see. Why wouldn't she make a wish?

That night I slept early, woke late. That night she never slept, never woke. Of course, I lay there above her in my own ill-fitting bunk looking down at her speculatively, willing her to wake up, wishing her a long sleep, till a doctor summoned by the hostel's manager came in and picked her wrist and shook his head. He studied me, unsure how I was related to her and gauging the level of my grief—did I need sedatives, a brotherly hand on the back? He said he would soon let me know the cause of death. I snorted. Spare me the details. Everyone dies of something.

12

COLLEGE REFRESHED ME. Back in the same class but classmates new. The scandal now a year old, overlapped by other scandals. The regret of not loving that girl soon replaced by the regret of not loving any girl.

Nena I forgot, as we do our hands and legs, or anything that doesn't merit a special effort to mentally retain. Life clears up old mysteries with new. Her condition had a name by now, *aquagenic urticaria*, a dermatological condition that prevented her from hydration; she was no witch who had accidentally cursed herself. Only someone with skin issues.

There had been a letter in her belongings for me. I'd felt that first stab of suspicion then, that this had all been planned meticulously by her. She always intended us to reach the city of my college by her last hour, timed it so.

I read her letter, as rambling as anything she ever said.

I know I call you Tata and that's not your name,

but a name I call you because it is my name for you and the name only I call you. Remind me sometime to tell you the Aztec tale about this couple Tata and Nena who run here and there when Rain God Tlaloc floods the world and there's just too much water...

That night out with Tash she asked me if we were, you know, more than just travel companions. I was at a loss for words. I kicked myself for not having seen it coming. You are not my son or nephew, not my flesh, not my blood, and Tash only asked what anyone would ask. I did think for a minute of telling her what we were, that there are other journeys between men and women. Equally, if not more, important. But then I thought if she had missed out on the platonic all her life, who am I to make her feel the lack? Better she go away thinking this some tawdry transactional affair than understand such a random connect. I mean what can be more connected than two people travelling in the same direction just because they want to. If you promised me the moon we'd have lasted but a night. Moon gone, we gone.

*I remember you hovering in my doorway that first time, not listening to a grovelling word your mother was saying. And I thought, '*Vouse et nul autre.*' You and no one else. I had a year to live, you had a year to give. Ah, fate can count.*

I set out to taste water, and I drank rain straight from the sky. As for my search for a descendent—can't

I pass you off, all of you and no one but you, as mine and only mine? I leave you my stories to tell and my house to sell.

Last things last. Burn me, turn me to ash, pour me in the stream where my every book flows.

~

I stroke vanishing plumes of smoke like pony necks. I curse verse, I bless verse. I laugh, I cry, I cry, I laugh, my neighbours move cities. I travel to other lands, to meet other poets, to read from my work, to collaborate with musicians. I compose aria, jingles and jagged odes to her. She who

loosened her grip on sky above, earth below, her share of air and people,

bade bye to setting sun, waning moon, moaning wind, rain with its two left feet,

she, a white spot I rub my eye to see.

I remember how in the crammed aisle of a flight she had summarised 'us' in German words, words I understand today as a cry between any two people on this bewildering planet—'Let's speak with each other though we don't share a common language.'

Yes, let's, my quiet now yours.

~

The man I never wanted to be has become me. He reminds me of orange peels and mothballs, of eucalyptus tea and bullets lodged in a mother's heart. How little we know of the men who make us till we wake up as them. An old man has taken my place, a father figure, a mentor, an ad for the brotherhood of men, ho ho ho. I impersonate me. Whispering against my father's whisper of 'not my son'—'Father, it's me.'

In slim volumes of my poetry I sign my name with exaggerated modesty, both Ts lower case: tata. Women like poets. They like us drunk and depressed. And, like I found out very young, read indifference all wrong. I get letters all the time, declarations of eternal love and threats of slit wrists. At the last reading, I fractured my foot in the stampede. I am an old man, but they take my rheumy eyes for a brokenness they think only they can fix. If I look at anyone too long, getting my aged eyes to focus, they claim I'd seen their soul, their underwear; they blush and stammer, break into inane chatter, send me nude pictures that my sensible sweet secretary puts in the shredder, murmuring with pleasure, here go their breasts, their thighs, their necks...in her sensible sweet voice. They'd run away with me, I only have to ask. Sometimes it is all I can do, think of the woman I will never meet, never love, never die for.

~

'There are two kinds of regrets; doing what we did and not doing what we didn't. The latter somehow feels the lesser of the two.' Nena's words that night with Tash went to my head and how, a last-minute reprieve from the gallows. And then I thought how weak can I get? In the context of a young girl bestially mauled, to compare it to my own inaction, lack of will—but I had sighted a glimmer of hope for myself in those words; maybe, just maybe I wasn't to blame. I tasted redemption at the back of my throat. I couldn't help who I was. Bodies disobey. Mine was a mule.

So I got drunk. I felt as if Nena knew, that she always knew. Her eyes had been so kind, so listening, the next morning when she had told me they found me by the sea, babbling about poems drowning in the waves, never to surface again. My words can't swim, I had sobbed. Poets are easily sentimental, swamped by all that sadness at the beauty that passes by so shockingly swift, but at that time all I wanted was to stay untouched by the tragic that I inherently sensed in anything the least exquisite. Blindfolded, I'd followed her. By keeping my head down I hoped to bypass life. Shh, you never saw me.

I had felt it rise in me of course, on that day far, far away. The numbness. The nothing, the no, the never of me. *Whom will my death kill?* No one, not a one, now that you ask. Not even me. And now that I know, why not die? The water seemed a soothing bier, here to take me there. Waves licked my ankles with a delicate tongue. It was the sea come for my soul.

But sinking's not easy, I who was not soluble.

Hands, have to be her hands, pull me back, hug me close, call me friend, take me home, tuck me into bed. I almost died, she almost died. Insane water up in nose and eyes, stinging, *non compos mentis*...That was how she fell sick, I begin to realise whenever the alcohol recedes, that's how she died. Jumping in after me to sieve me from sea. Old handing over baton to Young. All those stories, all those breathless words, all that voice modulation, for stupid, stupid me.

The past in tumble-wash. I reverse memories, tell myself she fell into bed comatose when we reached Berlin, but maybe...mmmm...it was later, after my dip in the sea. But no sea in Berlin, the nearest harbour five hours away—I did check. Could be the Schlachtensee lake...Where O where did I suddenly spy the sea? Dates, dates, who knows when is when? No calendar on the wall, no clock. She died of damp, that much I know, seaweed in her lung.

Life ends—but death?

~

At the time I was traipsing around with Nena, growing older had just been a possibility among many possibilities. It was up to me, I thought, to stay young as long as I wanted.

Tipping her remains into that blueness had been fatal to me. That was the day life found me, defrosted me, and set up the decay of time in me. Clocks clawed out my heart and reset its beat. I started to age, to go sour.

I stood in all my lankiness, urn in hand, holding her for the first and the last time, pole-axed by the air I breathe, the breeze that blew, the first time aware of a feeling, even if it was loss.

Acknowledgements

THE OLD ARAB tale in this book is a retelling of a story I once heard. Heartfelt thanks to the unknown and original writer of this wise little lore.

I am grateful to Renuka Chatterjee, who read multiple drafts with exquisite care during the edits. And to Preeti Gill, the sanest of literary agents.